KT-482-727

From the family wedding of Victoria and Albert
to the spectacular marriage ceremony of Anne
and Mark, *Britain's Royal Brides* is a delightful
record of love and marriage in the grand style.
Here we have Queen Victoria's own account of
Princess May's wedding, and follow the Duke of
York's determined courtship of the lovely Lady
Elizabeth Bowes-Lyon, now the Queen Mother.
We learn of Princess Elizabeth, aged 13,
meeting her cousin and future husband, Philip,
for the first time, and are introduced to the
sophisticated life of Princess Margaret which led
to her marriage to Anthony Armstrong-Jones.
Finally, there is the glittering splendour of
Princess Anne's wedding, watched by five
hundred million people around the world.
Their stories are a part of the fabric of our
history and their wedding albums reflect a
tradition no longer seen in any other country.

Britain's Royal Brides

JOSY ARGY and WENDY RICHES

SPHERE BOOKS LIMITED
30/32 Gray's Inn Road, London WC1X 8JL

First published in Great Britain by David and Charles (Publishers) Ltd 1975
Copyright © JWP Publishing Limited 1975
Published by Sphere Books 1977

TRADE
MARK

This book is sold subject to the condition that
it shall not, by way of trade or otherwise, be lent,
re-sold, hired out or otherwise circulated without
the publisher's prior consent in any form of
binding or cover other than that in which it is
published and without a similar condition
including this condition being imposed on the
subsequent purchaser.

Set in Linotype Baskerville

Printed in Great Britain by
Hazell Watson & Viney Ltd
Aylesbury, Bucks

CONTENTS

To Sophie

ACKNOWLEDGEMENTS

We are grateful for the gracious permission of the Queen to republish passages from various printed sources, of which the copyright in the original text belongs to Her Majesty.

We would also like to thank the following authors, editors and publishers for permission to quote from their books:

George Allen & Unwin Ltd for *Queen Mary*, by James Pope-Hennessy; Constable & Co Ltd for *Queen Alexandra*, by Georgina Battiscombe; Evans Brothers Ltd for *Dearest Mama*, edited by Roger Fulford, and for *My Memories of Six Reigns*, by Princess Marie Louise; Robert Hale & Co for *Thirty Years a Queen*, by Geoffrey Wakeford; Hamish Hamilton Ltd for *Queen Victoria, Her Life and Times*, Vol I, by Cecil Woodham-Smith; Hodder & Stoughton Ltd for *Queen Elizabeth the Queen Mother*, by Dorothy Laird; Holt, Rinehart & Winston, and Frederick Muller Ltd, for *Victoria, Albert and Mrs Stevenson*, edited by Edward Boykin; Macmillan (London) Ltd for *King George VI*, by John W. Wheeler-Bennett, *The Youthful Queen Victoria*, by Dormer Creston, and *The Prince Consort*, by Roger Fulford; John Murray (Publishers) Ltd for *Edward VII*, by Philip Magnus, *My Dear Duchess*, edited by A. L. Kennedy, and *Letters of Queen Victoria*, Vol II, edited by George Earle Buckle; Nigel Nicolson for *King George V*, by Harold Nicolson; and Weidenfeld & Nicolson Ltd for *Victoria R.I.*, by Elizabeth Longford.

ACKNOWLEDGEMENTS TO ILLUSTRATIONS

The illustrations in this volume are reproduced by courtesy of the following:

By gracious permission of Her Majesty the Queen, plates 5, 14, 33; Camera Press Ltd, plates 24, 29, 39, 40, 43, 44, 45; John Freeman, plates 7, 8; Keystone Press Agency Ltd, plate 37; London Museum, plates 7, 8; Mansell Collection, plates 2, 25; Mary Evans Picture Library, plate 18; Popperfoto, plates 36, 38, 47; Radio Times Hulton Picture Library, plates 6, 9, 15, 19, 30, 32, 34, 35; Royal Archives, Windsor, plates 10, 11, 12, 13, 16, 17, 20, 22, 23; Syndication International, plates 26, 31, 41, 42, 46; The Times, plates 27, 28.

INTRODUCTION

The British royal wedding, as we know it today, is a twentieth-century phenomenon. Princess Anne's widely televised marriage ceremony was only the tenth royal wedding celebrated in Westminster Abbey in its 900-year history. The first recorded royal marriage to be held in the Abbey was that of Henry I to Matilda, daughter of the King of Scotland, on 11 November 1100. For the most part later royalty tended to wed privately in their royal chapels. Even the weddings of Victoria, Alexandra and Mary, despite the illuminations and decorations in the streets, were largely family affairs, as is illustrated by contemporary prints.

Today, colour television has robbed the event of most of its privacy, if of none of its grandeur, and turned it into a one-day royal operetta with world-wide distribution. All the world loves a royal bride, and the uniquely British pageantry of the occasion – the glass coaches, the Guardsmen in their scarlet and gold, the massed bands in the streets and the solemn ceremonial in the Abbey.

In tracing the path to the altar of seven royal brides – five Queens of England and two royal princesses – we offer no startling revelations, no *secrets d'alcôve*; but history is a marvellous spinner of tales and the plots could hardly be improved upon. Some are dramatic, some romantic, some have a happy ending, others are tinged with tragedy. All are fascinating for the complex interplay of reasons of state, family considerations, royal traditions, human emotions and the strange hand of Fate. Like an intricate court tapestry, motifs and figures weave in and out of the various reigns. The small figure of Victoria, that royal matriarch, dominates the scene. We see her enthroned in the place of honour at the wedding of the lovely Alexandra to her son Bertie; and thirty years later, stouter and seemingly smaller, at the marriage of the shy Princess May to the Duke of York. Whether for luck or sentiment,

9

myrtle grown from Victoria's bouquet is still tucked into the flowers at a royal wedding. It formed part of the flower arrangements at Princess Elizabeth's wedding breakfast, and her daughter Anne carried a few sprigs in her bouquet.

There are some fascinating coincidences. The infant Victoria and Albert were delivered by the same midwife. Princess May was born in the same apartments at Kensington Palace as Queen Victoria, on almost the same day in May, and she was given two chances of becoming Queen. There was the case, too, of a father and son with a similar destiny: both were Dukes of York, neither expected to reign but one became George V and the other George VI – by the grace of God, in dramatic circumstances. Then there were the proposals, the wedding gifts, the bridal dresses – some yellowed like old prints, some relegated to that no man's land of fashion, too old to be chic, not old enough for charm. And the marriage ceremonies, the honeymoons: Victoria's hasty three days at Windsor and back to the engrossing business of being Queen; May's rather gloomy stay at Sandringham in the rain, with her mother-in-law dropping in for breakfast; Anne cruising in the Caribbean and dancing with the crowds in the streets in Ecuador.

CHAPTER ONE.

VICTORIA AND 'DEAREST ALBERT'

At 4 o'clock on the morning of 24 May 1819 a German midwife by the name of Fraulein Siebold delivered a baby girl in a large room in Kensington Palace, overlooking the Round Pond. Three months later the same midwife had travelled to a small castle romantically situated in the middle of a German forest, to attend the birth of a rather frail baby boy. Fraulein Siebold had carved a small niche for herself in history; for the two babies, linked by blood ties, were Victoria and Albert. Although they were not to meet for another sixteen years, their marriage was already being discussed by their families when they were hardly out of the cradle.

Their story, which started, so unromantically, as a political gambit to further the Coburg family fortunes, was to turn into a tale of almost legendary devotion – the very epitome of virtuous Victorian marriage at a court which had been better known for its debauchery than its domestic ambience. The marriage, distrusted by the English Parliament and disliked by the people, was to lay the foundations of the most popular dynasty in British history and to change the whole concept of nineteenth-century monarchy in Europe.

Alexandrina Victoria was a strapping, energetic, corn-haired baby. Her father, the Duke of Kent, was the fourth son of George III. Her mother, Victoire, was the daughter of the Duke of Saxe-Coburg-Saalfeld, and the widow of the elderly Prince of Leiningen. Despite this sizeable infusion of German blood, Victoria, with her beautiful fair skin and large blue eyes, was the picture of an English baby. 'How pretty the little Mayflower will be when I manage to see her,' her German grandmother, the Dowager Duchess of Coburg, wrote dotingly to her daughter the Duchess of Kent just after Albert's birth. 'Siebold cannot say often enough what a lovely little darling she is.'[1] The little darling, though affectionate and easy to amuse, was uncommonly obstinate and self-willed for one so young and indulged in outbursts of truly Hanoverian temper.

Unlike the robust young Victoria, her cousin in Coburg, sonorously christened Francis Charles Augustus Albert Emmanuel, was a pale, anaemic child, constantly in poor health. His first diary, started at the age of five, contains a painstaking list of all his childish ailments. Bedevilled by sleepiness, he would disappear for hours – to be found by his nurse fast asleep in some quiet corner of the castle. Years later, as a young man at Victoria's court, he was to suffer agonies, trying to keep awake during the constant round of balls and late nights.

Although Albert looked back on his childhood as a happy time and upon The Rosenau, his father's summer residence in the forest as a paradise, his early years were shadowed by the loss of his pretty and doting young mother. When he was four, his father banished and later divorced the Duchess Louise for adultery. The charming and lively daughter of the rich Duke of Saxe-Gotha, she was married at the age of sixteen to Duke Ernest of Coburg, a man more than twice her age, debauched and boorish, who ill-treated and neglected her. After Albert's birth she consoled herself with lovers – none too discreetly – and as the little boy bore no resemblance to either his father or his elder brother, there were rumours that the process of consolation might have started earlier. It has been suggested that Albert's father was the Duke's younger brother, Leopold, who later, as King of the Belgians, was to play a major role in furthering the match between Victoria and Albert.

Albert was never allowed to see his mother again. She remarried but died tragically of cancer at an early age. There is a touching story that Louise, disguised as a peasant woman, returned to Coburg during a local festival to see her boys just once more by mingling with the crowd in the main square.

Albert was a clever and painstaking little boy, growing up in a world of men, devoted to his severe father, his brother and his tutor, Herr Florschütz. All his life he was to be more at home with men than with women, happier in the country than in cities, a student by temperament, bored by small talk and worldly pursuits. At eleven he wrote in his diary: 'I intend to train myself to be a good and useful man.'[2] There can be few childish promises that have been more fully honoured by the man.

While Albert was living his well-regulated life of study and out-door pursuits, the young Victoria, 'immured' within the Palace at Kensington, longed for fun and laughter and the company of young people. Her father the Duke of Kent had died when she was eight months old, leaving his wife to cope with a mountain of debts and the responsibility of bringing up the heir apparent to the throne of England.

Unlike Albert, Victoria had no illusions about her stifling and restricted childhood. 'Never had a room to myself till I was nearly grown up – always slept in my Mother's room till I came to the Throne.'[3] she wrote succinctly, describing what her half-sister Feodore more graphically called their 'imprisonment', without 'one cheerful thought in that dismal existence of ours.'[4]

But a measure of comfort and affection was provided by the de-voted care of Louise Lehzen, the daughter of a Lutheran clergy-man from a small village in Hanover, who was governess first to Feodore and later to Victoria. Created a Hanoverian baroness by George IV, she remained close to the Queen and influenced her greatly until her marriage.

Victoria's mentor and father-figure was her uncle, Leopold, King of the Belgians. Their long correspondence is full of sermonising advice on his part, affectionate enthusiasm on hers. From her let-ters and the pages of her Journal, which she started at the age of eleven, emerges a vivid picture of the young girl growing up in the shadow of the throne.

There was not much amusement in the life of the little figure walking the corridors of Kensington Palace, a piece of holly often pinned to the collar of her dress to make her keep her chin up. 'I am to-day fourteen years old. How very old! !'[5] reads a gloomy entry in her Journal. But she was eager to find pleasure in the things she loved – riding, opera, the ballet and dancing. At the ball given by King William IV and Queen Adelaide in honour of her fourteenth birthday, she danced quadrille after quadrille. 'We came home at half past twelve,' she writes glowingly. 'I was *very* much amused.'[6]

The high spots of her young life were the visits to England of her uncle Leopold and his second wife Louise, a daughter of King

Louis-Philippe of France. Only seven years older than Victoria, she loaded her with presents from Paris – evening dresses, hats, ribbons, cravats and tippets. She even sent her hairdresser to arrange the young Princess's hair in more fashionable style.

Victoria was no beauty. With her smooth, rosy-skinned face, pale brown hair and rather prominent blue eyes, she had an air of 'indecisive prettiness'. Her greatest charms were her clear silvery voice and her smile. 'No smile was the least like it,' wrote a contemporary, 'no shadow of it is preserved for posterity in any of her published likenesses.'[7]

Whatever her looks, the Princess was the greatest catch in Europe and there were many foreign princelings who cast covetous eyes in her direction. One of them was the tall young Duke of Orleans, brother of the Queen of the Belgians. In 1833 he travelled to England specially to see Victoria. But although he was to tell his sister that her little niece was a darling he found her too tiny. The people of Paris would rock with laughter at seeing them side by side, he told Louise.

The Duke was followed by his brother, the gay and attractive Louis de Nemours. Victoria found him delightful, but her suitor was put off by seeing her downing three plates of soup in succession.

Prince Christian of Schleswig-Holstein-Sonderburg-Glucksburg, a nephew of the King of Denmark, was half in love with Victoria, but nothing came of it and they were not to meet again until many years later, when by a quirk of fate his daughter Alexandra was about to marry Victoria's son, the Prince of Wales.

Very susceptible to male beauty, Victoria was intent on making a love match. She had been greatly struck by her cousin, Alexander Mensdorff Pouilly, the son of Princess Sophia of Saxe-Coburg; but Uncle Leopold, ever watchful, with Albert waiting in the wings, did not want her to fall in love with the wrong cousin. He wrote Victoria a rather deprecating letter about the young man.

Perhaps the greatest potential threat to Leopold's plans was William IV's determination to marry Victoria to one of the sons of the Prince of Orange, the eldest son of the King of the Netherlands, a Protestant and traditional ally of England. In 1836 the King invited the Prince of Orange and his two sons to Britain.

Alarmed, the Duchess of Kent sent her brother, the Duke of Coburg and his sons an invitation for Victoria's seventeenth birthday. King William was furious and even tried to stop the visit, saying he would not allow the young men to live under the same roof as the Princess. But the Duchess refused to give way.

As it was, the arrival of the Princes of Orange left Victoria cold. Queen Adelaide gave a ball in their honour at St James's Palace, but the Princess has left no record of having enjoyed the evening, and danced only five times. A few days later she wrote to King Leopold: 'The boys are very plain ... they look heavy, dull and frightened and are not at all prepossessing. So much for the *Oranges*, dear Uncle.'[8]

She was not to be so off-hand about the visit of her Coburg cousins. The two young men and their father arrived on 18 May 1836. Albert was a rather plump, studious boy of sixteen. He had been terribly seasick in crossing the Channel, had trouble with his English and found the late nights, the rich food and the social whirl of the Palace not to his taste.

But Victoria was delighted with her cousins, finding them 'very amiable, very kind and good and extremely merry, just as young people ought to be'.[9] She was particularly struck with Albert, whom she thought 'extremely handsome; his hair is about the same colour as mine (a light brown) his eyes are large and blue, and he has a beautiful nose and a very sweet mouth with fine teeth; but the charm of his countenance is his expression, which is most delightful; *c'est à la fois* full of goodness and sweetness, and very clever and intelligent'.[10]

Albert was less starry-eyed about his English cousin, and in the middle of letters home complaining incessantly about the late nights, he merely describes her as 'very agreeable'.

There was no talk of love on this first visit. We have the Prince's own account of it. 'We stayed from 3–4 weeks at Kensington, Princess Victoria and myself, both at the age of 17, were much pleased with each other, but not a word in allusion to the future passed either between us, or with the Duchess of Kent.'[11]

Victoria, with characteristic warmth was deeply saddened by the departure of the cousins. She wrote to Uncle Leopold about Albert: 'he possesses every quality that could be desired to make

15

me perfectly happy ... I have only now to beg you, my dearest Uncle, to take care of the health of one, now so dear to me ...'[12] Her Journal received even more passionate outpourings. 'It was our last *happy happy* breakfast with this dear Uncle and these *dearest* beloved Cousins, whom I *do* love so *very very* dearly, much more dearly than any others cousins in the *world*.'[13]

The cousins were not to meet again for nearly three years. In that time they had led very different lives. Albert, a student at Bonn University with his brother, toured Switzerland and Italy, like many a well-born young man of his age. Victoria may not have found a place in his heart, yet, but she was certainly on his mind. He filled an album with views of the places they visited and other mementoes and sent it to her. Years later, the widowed, grieving Queen was to take it with her wherever she went as her most treasured possession.

Victoria's life had taken a far more dramatic turn – with the death of King William IV, she found herself Queen of England at the age of eighteen. From being supervised every minute of the day and night she was now gloriously free. After her penny-pinching childhood she was rich, with a Civil List of £385,000 a year for life and the income from the Duchies of Lancaster and Cornwall amounting to over £60,000 each, although in 1841 the income from the Duchy of Cornwall passed to the Prince of Wales. In a typical gesture, the Queen immediately set aside £50,000 to pay off her father's debts.

Almost overnight she exchanged the company of Lehzen and the small talk of women for the society of sophisticated men of the world, particularly that courtly, witty and charming old statesman, Lord Melbourne. The relationship between the inexperienced eager girl of eighteen and her Prime Minister has all the elements of an *amitié amoureuse*.

At fifty-eight, William Lamb, Viscount Melbourne, was still a captivating man. An aristocrat with striking good looks and a fine and original mind, an accomplished classical scholar, with a whimsical sense of humour, he talked about things Victoria had never discussed before and he brought history and famous people vividly to life for her. He learned to curb his tendency to utter picturesque oaths and became the perfect combination of devoted courtier and father-figure to 'her little majesty'.

She, on her side, always asked for his opinion, even when she wore a new dress or changed her hairstyle. 'Asked Lord M if he liked my dress, a cherry-coloured silk, with a magnificent old lace flounce ... The dress I had on the day before, a striped one, he didn't think ugly, but said it was like the pattern of a sofa.'[14]

We are indebted to Sallie Stevenson, the wife of the American Minister to the Court of St James, for some vivid pen-pictures of the Queen in those early days of her reign. 'Only imagine,' she wrote to her family in America, 'a young creature, just 18 brought up in retirement & seclusion suddenly finding herself sovereign of the greatest Kingdom of the Earth ... She seems to have turned the heads of the young & old & it is amazing to hear those grave & dignified ministers of state talking of her as a thing not only to be admired but to be adored.'[15]

The wife of the British Ambassador to Paris, Lady Granville, describes her as 'such a little love of a Queen.' Little indeed, for the Queen was tiny, under five feet and obviously concerned about it. She moaned to Lord Melbourne, 'everybody grows but me'.[16] Yet her lack of height combined with her natural dignity created a charm all her own. Lord Holland wrote to Lord Granville in Paris: 'Well, I have been to Court ... and I am come back quite a courtier and a bit of a lover, for her manner and demeanour deserve all that is said of them.'[17]

Small wonder that in the midst of all this adulation the image of the studious young cousin from Coburg began to fade ... Lord Melbourne also did not seem too enthusiastic about Albert. The Germans smoked too much and did not wash their faces, he told Victoria half humorously – 'cousins are not a very good thing and those Coburgs are not popular abroad'.[18]

Like her great predecessor, Queen Elizabeth, Victoria began to toy with the idea of not marrying and played for time. She wrote to Uncle Leopold with a string of excuses, she was too young ... Albert was too young ... he should improve his English, himself, his knowledge of the world ...

On his side, Albert was getting distinctly nervous about the whole situation. He confided his fears to Uncle Leopold. 'If after waiting perhaps two or three years, I should find the Queen no longer desired the Marriage, it would place me in a ridiculous position ... and would ruin my prospects for the future.'[19] To please the young Queen, Albert reluctantly accepted the edict that he must go to Italy to complete his education. Bitterly he wrote to his tutor, 'I am to go into society, learn the ways of the world and vitiate my culture with fashionable accomplishments.'[20]

By the summer of 1839, with the glory of her coronation behind her, the wear and tear of monarchy were beginning to take their toll of Victoria's looks and temper. She had attacks of depression, was short-tempered with her ladies and even with Lord M. She was losing the flower-like looks of her youth and was putting on weight. She was weighed and found 'to my horror' that she was 8 stone 13 lb – 'an incredible weight for my size.'[21] Lord M often told her that she ate too much, drank too much beer and did not walk enough. Marriage was on her mind, but not in the way her Uncle Leopold desired. She was to write about this period: 'I dreaded the thought of marrying ... I was so accustomed to have my own way that I thought it was 10 to 1 that I shouldn't agree with anybody.'[22]

In the summer she wrote a letter to Leopold which spelled out her state of mind. 'I am anxious to put several questions to you ... First of all ... if Albert is aware of the wish of his *Father* and *you* relative to *me*? Secondly, if he knows that there is no *engagement* between us? I am anxious that you should acquaint Uncle Ernest, that if I should like Albert, that I can make *no final promise this year* ... I may not have the *feeling* for him which is requisite to ensure happiness. I *may* like him as a friend, and as a *cousin* and as a *brother*, but not more ... and should this be the case I am very anxious that it should be understood that I am not guilty of any breach of promise, for I *never gave any*.'[23]

This letter must have come as a shock to Leopold, but in his careful and patient way he merely held Victoria to her promise to receive her Coburg cousins in the autumn of 1839.

The Queen's feelings towards her cousins were not much warmer by the autumn. She wrote tartly to Leopold from Windsor Castle. 'I had a letter from Albert yesterday saying they could not set off, he thought before the 6th ... I think they don't exhibit much *empressement* to come here ... which rather shocks me. The sooner they come the better. I have got the house *full* of Ministers.'[24]

The young Queen's displeasure was to be swept away by the impact of Albert's appearance at Windsor Castle on 10 October. The Prince arrived pale as a wax candle, after yet another ghastly Channel crossing, but even hours of sea-sickness could not detract from his striking good looks. The immature boy had turned into a young Apollo of rare beauty and elegance. The doubts, the reservations of the last year vanished and Victoria wrote in her Journal that night: 'It was with some emotion that I beheld Albert who is beautiful ... such beautiful blue eyes, an exquisite nose and such a pretty mouth with delicate mustachios and slight, but very slight whiskers; a beautiful figure, broad in the shoulders and a fine waist.'[25]

Albert, who had come determined to withdraw if the Queen did not make up her mind, was so nervous that he did not sleep during his first few nights at the Castle. He was not to wait long. Two days after he arrived, the Queen sent him a message through Lehzen and his equerry, saying that the Prince had made 'a very favourable impression' on her. At the same time she wrote to Uncle Leopold: 'The dear cousins arrived at half-past seven on Thursday, after a very bad and almost dangerous passage, but looking both well and much improved ... Albert's *beauty is most striking*, and he is so amiable and unaffected – in short very *fascinating ...*'[26]

On 15 October, Victoria called Albert to her little Blue Closet and offered him 'her hand and her heart'. We have both the young people's accounts of the scene. First, Albert's more concise description in a letter to Baron Stockmar. 'I am writing to you today on one of the happiest days of my life to send you the most joyful possible news. Yesterday in a private audience V. declared her love for me and offered me her hand, which I seized in both mine and pressed tenderly to my lips. She is so good and kind to me that I can scarcely believe such affection should be mine ... For the present the event is to remain a secret ... what grieves me is that my aunt [Duchess of Kent] ... is not to know of it. But as everyone says she cannot keep her mouth shut and might even make bad use of the secret if it were entrusted to her I quite see the necessity of it . . . V. wishes that the wedding should take place as early as the beginning of February to which I gladly agreed as the relations between a betrothed pair when the fact is public property may often appear indelicate.'[27]

Victoria's outpourings in her Journal are infinitely more passionate: 'Oh! to *feel* I was, and am, loved by *such* an Angel as Albert was *too great delight to describe!* He is *perfection* . . . I told him I was quite unworthy of him and kissed his dear hand . . . I really felt it was the happiest brightest moment in my life . . . I feel the happiest of human beings.'[28]

Writing immediately to Uncle Leopold, with the honesty which marked all her reactions, the Queen recalled the letter she had written to him earlier. 'My feelings are a *little* changed, I must say, since last Spring, when I said I couldn't *think* of marrying for *three or four years*: but seeing Albert has changed all this.'[29]

The Prince spent a month at Windsor. Happy days for the young couple – they exchanged rings and locks of hair, they rode, danced, played and sang together and finalised the wedding plans, deciding to follow the ceremonial for the marriage of George III and Queen Charlotte in the Chapel Royal in 1761.

The Queen confided to her Journal: 'We sit so nicely side by side on that little blue sofa; no two Lovers could ever be happier than we are! . . . He took my hands in his, and said my hands were so little he could hardly believe they *were* hands, as he had hitherto *only* been accustomed to handle hands like Ernest's.'[30]

The Duchess of Kent was finally told of the engagement on 10 November, four days before the Prince returned to Coburg. 'She took me in her arms and cried,' Victoria's Journal reports, 'and said, though I had not asked her, still that she gave her best blessing to it . . . I sent for dearest Albert, whom she embraced and said that she was as anxious for his happiness as for mine.'[31]

However, this happy state of affairs was short-lived. The Duchess, like many a widowed mother, wished to live at Buckingham Palace with her daughter after the marriage – which, in the Queen's words, 'we agreed *never* would do.' The Duchess complained bitterly to Albert that she was being turned out of the house by her daughter. It was the first of many irritations, both private and public, which were to mar the four months of the royal engagement.

In Coburg, Albert was 'lost in bewilderment', as he wrote to his future mother-in-law: 'What a multitude of emotions of the most diverse kind sweeps over and overwhelms me – hope, love for dear Victoria; the pain of leaving home, the parting from very dear kindred, the entrance into a new circle of relations, prospects most brilliant, the dread of being unequal to my position ... I pack, arrange, give directions about pieces of property, settle contracts, engage servants, write an infinitude of lettters, study the English Constitution and occupy myself about my future.'[32]

In London, the Queen summoned the Privy Council to announce her decision to marry Albert. She was so nervous that her hand trembled as she held the paper but she read the declaration in the 'clear, sonorous sweet-toned' voice which was one of her chief charms.

The marriage was not to prove popular with the country. The Prince was regarded as a penniless fortune-hunter and a foreigner to boot. A scurrilous rhyme much in favour ran:

He comes the bridegroom of Victoria's choice.
The nominee of Lehzen's vulgar voice:
He comes to take 'for better or for worse'
England's fat Queen and England's fatter purse.[33]

A rumour spread that Albert was a Catholic, as no mention of his religion had been made in the Queen's declaration of marriage. No sooner was this squashed, than a row broke out over the question of Albert's precedence – the Queen wanted him to rank after her, and before her uncles the royal dukes. The bitterest blow to the Queen and her future husband was Parliament's action in reducing the allowance for the Prince from the £50,000 a year which had been asked for to a mere £30,000. The Prince was 'shocked and exasperated by the disrespect of the thing.'[34]

But feeling ran very high in the country and *The Times* thundered piously: 'The horse he rides is from the Royal stables. The book he reads is from the library of the palace. Every accommodation, every luxury of human life starts up for this fortunate, and, we are willing to hope, this accomplished and estimable youth, without cost or trouble. The demand therefore for Prince Albert of £50,000 is among the most indecorous proposals that could be made to Parliament.'

Albert had to suffer two more defeats before his marriage – this time at the hands of his loving Victoria. He lost the battle to appoint his own household – he wanted a group of high-minded, non-political Germans. 'As to your wish about your gentlemen, my dear Albert,' wrote the Queen, 'I must tell you quite honestly that it will not do. You may entirely rely upon me that the people who will be round you will be absolutely pleasant people of high standing and good character.'[35] His suggestion that the honeymoon, to be spent at Windsor, should last a week or two met with another rebuking letter from his bride-to-be. 'You forget, my dearest Love, that I am the Sovereign, and that business can stop and wait for nothing . . . it is quite impossible for me to be absent from London; therefore two or three days is already a long time to be absent.'[36] But mostly their correspondence was suitably lover-like.

'Dear, Splendid Victoria,' wrote Albert, 'even in my dreams I never imagined I should find so much love on earth.'

'Dearest beloved Albert,' wrote the Queen, 'I pray daily and nightly that I may become more worthy of you.'[37]

As the wedding day approached, there were some of the minor panics which afflict lesser mortals.

'I observe with horror that I have not formally invited your father,' Victoria wrote to Albert, some three weeks before the wedding, 'though that is a matter of course. My last letter will have set that right.'[38]

Six days before the wedding, Victoria was suffering from a dreadful cold and the kind of second thoughts which attack many brides. Was she making a mistake? 'I have always had my own way, suppose he should endeavour to thwart me and oppose me?'[39]

The Prince on his way to England was battling again with a dreadful Channel crossing. When he arrived at Buckingham Palace, where – against Melbourne's advice – he was to stay until the wedding, the young Queen's doubts were once more banished by his presence.

They exchanged gifts – a beautiful sapphire and diamond

brooch for the Queen, a diamond Garter and the Star and Badge of the Garter in diamonds for Albert. In the afternoon the Lord Chancellor administered the oath of naturalisation and that night there was a great dinner which Albert, still giddy from sea-sickness, and with his predilection for early nights can hardly have enjoyed.

The night before the wedding the couple spent an hour reading the marriage service and practising with the ring. At the Queen's request, the word 'obey' was retained in the marriage service.

The 10th of February dawned wet, dismal and blustery. 'The last time I slept alone,' the Queen's Journal reads. 'Got up at quarter to nine . . . having slept well and breakfasted at half past nine.'[40] Picking up her pen and a sheet of paper, Victoria wrote to Albert on her wedding morning:

'Dearest – how are you to-day, and have you slept well? I have rested very well and feel very comfortable to-day. What weather! I believe however, the rain will cease, Send one word, when you, my most dearly loved bridegroom, will be ready.'[41]

Unlike previous royal weddings which had taken place late at night, the ceremony was held at 1 pm. Some 300 guests, freezing cold and packed like sardines, waited in the Chapel Royal of St James's Palace. Without the benefit of either television or still cameras, the atmosphere of that day is conjured up for us by eye-witnesses.

Albert stood very handsome in the uniform of a field marshal, the Order of the Garter across his military-style tunic, a long tasselled sash swinging against his white knee breeches, a great white satin bow on each shoulder. Clasping a green velvet Bible and 'awkward with embarrassment', he waited for his bride, while the kindly Queen Adelaide hovered by his side, eager to help him in his nervousness. Close by stood Albert's father and brother and the Queen's uncles, the Dukes of Sussex and Cambridge.

At 12.30 the Queen left Buckingham Palace accompanied by her mother and her Mistress of the Robes, the beautiful Duchess of Sutherland, for the short journey to the Chapel. There she found her twelve bridesmaids, who had been securely locked in for ninety minutes, demure in the dresses of white tulle which the Queen herself had sketched for them.

There was a flourish of trumpets as the Queen walked up the aisle, with Lord Melbourne, who was wearing a splendid new coat which he said had been built like a 74-gun ship, carrying the Sword of State in the procession. The bride's train was too short for so many attendants and the bridesmaids were huddled together and could hardly move. Victoria's wedding dress has been described as a tasteless muddle. The tiny figure was lost in yards of satin and lace, covered with bows, orange blossom, the Order and Star of the Garter, 'my Turkish diamond necklace ... and Albert's beautiful sapphire brooch.'[42]

The Duke of Sussex gave his niece away and could not restrain his sobs which resounded round the small chapel. There were more tears on the face of the Duchess of Kent, who wore a shimmering dress of white and silver with a train of blue velvet and 'a disconsolated and distressed face'. Victoria's beloved governess, Louise Lehzen, looked handsome and striking in a black velvet Spanish hat, surmounted by a white plume.

The wife of the American Minister, with her vivid pen, gives us this description of the ceremony, after waiting 'two mortal hours of shivering' in the cold church.

'The deportment of the royal bride was really beautiful. It blended the sensibility of the woman with the dignity of the queen ... her agitation was only discoverable in the marble paleness of her brow and the shaking of the orange flowers. The Prince is very handsome and graceful and looks older than he is by several years. Both made the responses very audibly, but her tones, tho' soft and low, were yet so perfectly distinct that every one in the chapel heard her vow to love, honour and obey and when he promised to love and cherish her, she turned her sweet and innocent looks upon him with an expression that brought tears into every eye that saw it.'[43]

One of the bridesmaids wrote, in later years, that after the wedding they had found themselves in a room in St James's Palace with Victoria and Albert. 'An attendant brought in ... a cloth bag and gave it to the Queen, who drew from it, one at a time, a little dark blue velvet case, giving one to each of us.'[44] Inside each was a brooch designed by the Queen, a turquoise eagle with a ruby beak and pearl claws. The wedding breakfast at Buckingham Palace was a family affair. The Queen sat between her new husband and the Duke of Sussex. 'The wedding cake, which was admirably designed, was a great object of attraction. It was more than nine feet in circumference by 16 inches deep. Its weight was 300 pounds and the materials of which it was composed cost one hundred guineas. On the top of the cake was the figure of Britannia in the act of blessing the illustrious bride and bridegroom. The figures were nearly a foot in height and by the feet of the Prince was the effigy of a dog, intended to represent fidelity, while at the feet of the Queen were two turtle doves denoting the felicities of the marriage state. A cupid, beautifully modelled, was writing in a volume opened on his knees, the date and the day of the marriage and various cupids were disporting themselves after the manner of cupids.'[45]

In the afternoon, Victoria went upstairs to change, putting on 'a white silk gown, trimmed with swansdown, and a bonnet with orange flowers ... Dearest Albert came up and fetched me downstairs, when we took leave of Mamma and drove off at near 4, I and Albert alone.'[46]

They drove the three hours to Windsor 'in poor and shabby style', according to Charles Greville the diarist; 'instead of the new chariot in which most married people are accustomed to dash along they were in one of the old travelling coaches, with a small escort.'[47] But the whole city was splendidly illuminated, her subjects cheered her all along the road and when they reached Eton they were greeted by rockets and 550 noisy schoolboys!

At the Castle, the young couple looked over their rooms – the Prince noting, perhaps with foreboding, that Baroness Lehzen's room opened directly out of the Queen's dressing room. Having changed her dress, the Queen joined her bridegroom in his room, where he was playing the piano.

'We had dinner in our sitting-room,' her Journal tells us, 'but I had such a sick headache that I could eat nothing, and was obliged to lie down ... for the rest of the evening – but ill or not I *never*, *never*, spent such an evening. My dearest, dearest dear Albert sat on a footstool by my side and his excessive love and affection gave me feelings of heavenly love and happiness I never could have *hoped* to have felt before ... Oh, this was the happiest day of my life!'[48]

Next day they were up at half past eight – a fact which moved Charles Greville to complain to Lady Palmerston that the wedding night had been too short and was 'not the way to provide us with a Prince of Wales.'[49]

But the Queen had no complaints. She was in raptures at having 'Albert's beautiful angelic face' to greet her at breakfast. The Prince, wearing a black velvet jacket and no neckcloth, 'looked more beautiful than it is possible for me to say.'[50]

Next day it was Albert's turn to feel unwell, but by the evening he was sufficiently recovered to attend a dinner for ten given by the Queen. The following evening there was a great ball at Windsor, to the disgust of Lady Palmerston who thought it indelicate of the young couple not to spend some time in isolation. After midnight on the night of the ball the Queen went upstairs and found Albert sleeping soundly on the sofa in their bedroom, 'looking quite beautiful'.[51]

There is a degree of irony in discovering that Victoria, that symbol of propriety, should have started her married life by shocking some of her entourage. But it is doubtful if the rumblings of other people's opinion had any effect on the young Queen's happiness. Back in London, three days later, she exuded high spirits, as she told Lord Melbourne: 'I never could have thought there was such happiness in store for me.'[52] And she wrote to Uncle Leopold, who after all had made it all happen: 'I do not think it possible for anyone in the world to be happier, or as happy as I am.'[53]

In marrying Albert, Victoria had found what she described herself as her 'safe haven'. She was to emerge from it some twenty years later, tried by personal tragedy and the cares of state, a small stout Britannia – a great queen, in no small measure fashioned by the man she had loved so deeply.

CHAPTER TWO

QUEEN ALEXANDRA

Alexandra Caroline Marie Charlotte Louise Julia – usually shortened to Alix – was born on 1 December 1844. Her father, Prince Christian, was a captain in the Danish Guards at the time, but because of his royal connections the family lived in the Yellow Palace in Copenhagen. Despite its grand name, the Yellow Palace is not at all pretentious. It is a pleasant family house in a street full of similar houses, near the harbour. Here, Alix spent a happy childhood. Because of lack of space, she had to share a room with her younger sister Dagmar (who later married the Crown Prince of Russia) but they got on very well together and remained good friends all their lives. Alix had another sister, Thyra, who was much younger, and three brothers – Frederick, William and Waldemar.

Prince Christian's pay as a captain was small, and he and his wife found it hard to make ends meet with a large family. Consequently, the girls were encouraged to make their own clothes and knit their own stockings, and not much money was spent on the family education. Their mother taught the children music (Alix inherited a great love of music and a sweet voice from her) while their father looked after their physical education; they learnt English from an early age from their English nannies, and somehow picked up a working knowledge of German and French. Their only other instruction was in religion.

When Alix was eight years old, her father was designated heir to the Danish throne by an agreement between Russia, France, Prussia, Austria, Sweden and England called the London Protocol, which laid down the Danish boundaries. In fact Prince Christian was not the nearest living heir but he was the only male in the family who had not blotted his copybook morally or politically. He had remained loyal to his country during boundary disputes, and he was popular because he had a brave army record and because he was a man of good character – unlike the reigning monarch, Frederick VII. Frederick had produced no heirs from two marriages and had set up home with a vulgar former milliner. They lived a life punctuated by drunken parties and scandalous affairs in the official royal residence – the Amalienborg Palace – just down the road from Alix and her family.

Prince Christian's expectations did not alter his income, and the family had to scrimp and save as much as before. However, they were an unusually happy group, with a sense of unity that was to last all their lives. Most of the year they lived in the Yellow Palace, spending summer holidays at Bernstorff – a charming eighteenth-century hunting lodge just outside Copenhagen – and, every alternate year, making a family pilgrimage to Schloss Rumpenheim, on the Main, in Germany. This large house had been left to Alix's mother's family, the Hesse-Cassels, on condition that they foregathered there at least once every two years. The six children who had inherited Rumpenheim were spread across Europe, but they came, a somewhat dowdy collection of Royals, with more titles than money.

Alix was born beautiful, an asset which went on improving with age. An English visitor to Copenhagen in 1854 described her thus: 'we saw a go-cart drawn by a goat, which was led by a very smart-looking footman in green and gold livery, with another one behind. Someone who looked like a ladies' maid or nurse was walking beside the cart. Seated in the cart was the most beautiful little girl about eight years old wearing a little fur bonnet . . . she waved to us gaily as she went by.'[1]

She had blue eyes, and light brown hair. Her complexion – according to a later description by Queen Victoria – was 'very clear but not at all fair; she is much darker than our children; she looks brown near them'.[2] She had an excellent figure; slim but with a strong, athletic frame. She was a good rider and loved to dance.

Temperamentally, Alix was a happy child. Passionate and impulsive, unsophisticated but blessed with natural tact, delightfully honest and affectionate. She was not clever, and she suffered from two drawbacks that were to affect her when she joined the English Royal Family – she had no sense of time, which infuriated her husband, and she had inherited a sad deafness from her mother which started in a slight way but got much worse after a severe illness in her twenties.

Undoubtedly, beauty was Alix's chief asset – and ultimately this was what won her her future husband, Bertie, the Prince of Wales.

Bertie – Albert Edward – was Queen Victoria's eldest son, born in 1841, three years before Alix. In contrast to his bride-to-be, he had a difficult, frustrating childhood. His father, Albert the Prince Consort, was dedicated to duty and had unswervingly high principles; his mother, the Queen, was totally under Albert's influence (even after his death) and tended to regard Bertie as a poor shadow of his father.

Both parents wanted their eldest son to be *perfect*, and Bertie was subjected to a tough educational programme from the age of five, cut off from other children, and made to study for exceptionally long hours. He became prone to outbursts of blind fury, and sometimes passed out; the Queen and his father found these natural symptoms of stress very strange. Bertie, who was a pretty child with a generous nature, must have suffered from their lack of understanding and apparent lack of affection. Queen Victoria was wrapped up in her husband and her country; her attitude to her nine children is summed up by this letter which she wrote when Bertie was fifteen: 'Even here [Balmoral], when Albert is often away all day long, I find no especial pleasure or compensation in the company of the elder children ... and only very occasionally do I find the rather intimate intercourse with them either easy or agreeable ... Firstly, I only feel properly *à mon aise* and quite happy when Albert is with me; secondly, I am used to carrying on my many affairs quite alone; and then I have grown up all alone, accustomed to the society of adult (and never with younger) people.'[3]

Unlike his mother, Bertie was quick to show affection. One of the first friends he was 'allowed' was Charles Wynn-Carrington, chosen as companion to Bertie's younger brother, Affie, but who wrote later: 'I always liked the Prince of Wales far the best. He had such an open, generous disposition and the kindest heart imaginable. He was a very plucky boy and always ready for fun which often got him into scrapes.'[4]

Bertie's first serious scrape happened when he was a tall, handsome lad of sixteen, with curly hair and light-coloured eyes. Accompanied by four (hand-picked) Eton schoolboys of his age, and four adults, he was sent to study at Königswinter, on the Rhine. It was the young Prince's first trip abroad with companions of his own age. The second night, after an excellent dinner with plenty of wine, he was caught kissing a pretty girl. The story was hushed up by his tutors, who gave him a severe scolding, but it was a hint of scandals to come. All his life, Bertie was to find women irresistible, and to succumb happily to their charms without first considering the consequences.

Along with a taste for women, Bertie had a gourmet's love of good food. His father wrote to him at Oxford University to warn him against putting on weight and losing his looks from eating dishes 'which an experienced and prudent liver will carefully avoid'.[5] The Queen thought he should learn to part his hair 'in a less effeminate and girlish way'[6] if he was to impress the serious-minded professors. However, both parents acknowledged that Bertie worked hard at university, and Albert wrote to their eldest daughter Vicky (Bertie's senior by a year and already married to the Crown Prince of Prussia) to say that although Bertie might prefer good food to mental effort, 'he is very good-natured and does what he *has to do* very well.'[7]

By now, Bertie spoke three languages fluently – English, French and German; English with a guttural German twang on the 'r's. He rode to hounds, shot, fished, stalked deer, and knew a little about horse-racing. He played racquets and tennis. His father still saw to every detail of his education, and made sure that Bertie mixed with leading academics, but he was not cut out to be an intellectual – his *métier* lay in dealing with people as he proved on his first official visit. The trip to America and Canada was full of political problems, but Bertie was an outstanding success. The crowds loved his charm and boyish vitality and showed their appreciation in tumultuous welcomes. He returned home to rare praise from his parents. Queen Victoria wrote proudly to Vicky: 'He was immensely popular everywhere and really deserves the highest praise, which should be given him all the more as he was never spared any reproof.'[8]

Though Queen Victoria and Albert were pleased, they still felt that their son's natural exuberance should be curbed, and decided that an early marriage was the answer. In their eyes, Bertie's bride had to meet several requirements: she must be royal and a Protestant, and the match must bring political advantage. Queen Victoria also expected 'good looks, health, education, character, intellect, and a good disposition', coupled with a certain strength of character. Bertie, on the other hand, wished her to be attractive and insisted (as his mother had done before him) that he would marry only for love.

The Queen and Prince Consort enlisted Vicky's help in finding a bride for Bertie. Mother and daughter discussed and discarded many eligible European princesses: 'The Weimars – very nice girls but delicate and not pretty'; Princess Alexandrine of Prussia, 'poor Addy, *not* clever or pretty'; Princess Marie of Altenburg, 'shockingly dressed and always with her most disagreeable mother.'[9] As for Alexandra of Denmark, Victoria and Albert would not consider her at first. The Queen objected to her immoral relatives; the Prince Consort objected to her on political grounds since the Danes were at loggerheads with his native country over the Schleswig-Holstein territories. But lack of attractive alternatives forced them to consider Alix, and when news came through that the Russian Emperor had obtained her picture for his son the Queen was startled into action. She wrote immediately to Vicky for information and a picture of the young Danish princess. Vicky replied from Prussia: 'I send you now a photograph of Prince Christian's lovely daughter; I have seen several people who have seen her of late – and who give such accounts of her beauty, her charm, her amiability, her frank, natural manner and many excellent qualities. I thought it right to tell you all this in Bertie's interest, though I as Prussian cannot wish Bertie should ever marry her.'[10]

The Prince Consort declared that from the photograph he would marry her at once; and Queen Victoria, whilst lamenting 'she is who she is', acknowledged her to be 'outrageously beautiful'.[11] Prince Albert wrote to Vicky: 'If the match were more or less your work . . . it would open the way to friendly relations between you and the Danes, which might later be a blessing and of use to Germany.'[12]

31

The next step was for Vicky to engineer a meeting and report first-hand about Alix. She and her husband, Fritz, travelled to Strelitz where they 'happened' to meet the Danish Royal Family. 'I have never set eyes upon a sweeter creature than Princess Alix,' enthused Vicky to her mother, 'she is lovely!'[13]

The prospective young suitor, Bertie, was advised of the plans being hatched for him and Alix. He repeated his intention of marrying for love, and said he would like to meet Alix. Vicky arranged a secret meeting for later that year (1861) in Germany, under her supervision. In the meantime, Bertie fulfilled a lifetime's ambition by attending Army Camp at Curragh in Ireland. Free from stifling parental supervision, he indulged in a brief affair with an actress called Nellie Clifden whom his brother officers smuggled into camp. Little did he know that the scandal over this would rock his marriage prospects, and alienate him from his mother temporarily.

On 24 September, Vicky presented Alix to her brother before the altar of Speyer Cathedral, and under cover of admiring the frescoes with the Bishop, watched their reactions anxiously.

The next day, she wrote to Queen Victoria: 'The reverse of indifference on both sides soon became quite unmistakable ... I felt very nervous the whole time, but ... I see that Alix has made an impression on Bertie, though in his own funny and undemonstrative way. He said to me he had never seen a young lady who pleased him so much ... She talked to him first, in her simple and unaffected way. She was not shy. I never saw a girl of sixteen so forward for her age; her manners are more like twenty-four.'[14] Alexandra's composure was all the more remarkable since the first she had known of the meeting had been that morning when her mother made her go and change into her best outfit.

The two royal parties travelled to Heidelberg, where Bertie and Alix exchanged signed photos and farewells before going their separate ways: Alix and family to Rumpenheim; Bertie back to Balmoral where his parents were waiting with high hopes of an early engagement. To their surprise and disappointment, Bertie hedged. He qualified his enthusiasm for Alix with reluctance to rush into something he might regret later. Queen Victoria wrote testily to Vicky: 'Bertie is extremely pleased with her, but as for

1 Queen Victoria at about the time of her coronation,
by J. Bouvier

2 The Prince Consort, by John Partridge, 1840

3 (*below left*) The Queen on her favourite horse, Theron, 1840

4 (*right*) Dancing the polka with Prince Albert

5 (*below*) The marriage ceremony, by Hayter, 1840

6 'The Bridal Morn' by Lock

7 The bridal procession

8 A wedding portrait by Topham, engraving by Bradshaw

9 Princess Alexandra of Denmark

10 (*above*) Prince and
Princess Christian of
Denmark with their
daughters. Princess
Alexandra (*left*) and
Princess Dagmar, 1862

11 (*right*) The Prince of
Wales and Princess
Alexandra of Denmark,
September 1862

12 Princess Alexandra with her dog, December 1862

13 (*below*) Princess Helena (left), Louise and Beatrice (centre) in the clothes they wore at their brother's wedding

14 Detail from a portrait by Francis Frith of the marriage ceremony, 10 March 1863

15 Queen Victoria with the newlywed couple

16 A family group taken after the wedding. Front row (left to right) Princess Louise, Queen Victoria, Princess Beatrice, Princess of Wales, Prince Leopold. Back row (left to right) Princess Louise of Hesse, Prince Louis of Hesse, Prince of Wales, Princess Helena

17 At Sandringham shortly after the wedding

18 Princess Victoria May of Teck

19 May of Teck with her mother, the Duchess of Teck in 1870

20 (*below*) The Duke and Duchess of York with attendants, 6 July 1893

21 (*above left*) Artist's impression of the royal table at the wedding breakfast at Buckingham Palace

22 (*left*) The wedding presents at White Lodge, July 1893

23 (*above*) The Duke of York in a canoe on the lake near York Cottage

24 (*right*) Princess May of Teck, about 1855

25 Queen Mary, taken shortly after her coronation

being in love, I don't think he can be, or that he is capable of enthusiasm about anything in the world.'[15]

Within a month, the reason for Bertie's reluctance to commit himself became clear when the news of his affair with Nellie Clifden filtered through to London. Sadly for the Prince, the actress had not been able to resist bragging about her latest conquest. 'With a heavy heart upon a subject which has caused me the greatest pain I have yet felt in this life',[16] Albert wrote to ask his son if the rumours were true, and if this was the reason for his reluctance to marry. Bertie confessed at once and begged forgiveness, promising that the affair was at an end. Albert, heartbroken yet prepared to forgive, travelled to Cambridge for a reconciliation with his son.

Four days later, the Prince Consort wrote to Vicky: 'I am at a very low ebb. Much worry and great sorrow (about which I beg you not to ask questions) have robbed me of sleep during the past fortnight. In this shattered state I had a very heavy catarrh and for the past four days am suffering from headache and pains in my limbs which may develop into rheumatism.'[17] In fact these were typhoid symptoms and the Prince died less than three weeks later.

The doctors attributed his fatal illness to a germ from one of the Windsor drains, but Victoria – grief-stricken – laid the blame at Bertie's door for dragging his father's health down with worry. After the funeral, she couldn't bear to have her eldest son around – 'Bertie (oh! that Boy – much as I pity, I never can or shall look at him without a shudder)'[18] – so she arranged for him to tour Palestine and the Middle East for four and a half months.

While he was away, the Queen determined that he should marry as soon as possible; 'though the intentions are good, the tact, the head, the heart all are lamentably weak. The marriage is the thing . . .'[19] she wrote to Vicky, and charged her with investigating Alexandra's background.

Vicky's task was not made easy by a number of interfering busybodies who were politically opposed to an English–Danish alliance and stirred up rumours that Prince and Princess Christian were immoral; that Princess Christian had had an illegitimate child; that Alix had dallied with a young officer. When these charges failed to stick, they revived an old health scare about a mark on

Alix's neck that she had had since childhood. (Alix generally hid this blemish with her long ringlets; in later years, when she liked to pile her hair on her head, she started a fashion for wearing 'chokers' that lasted half a century.) Malicious tongues said this scar was due to scrofula, a disease indicating a tendency to tuberculosis; in fact it was the result of a doctor experimenting to cure a common cold.

In June, Bertie came home from his travels. His mother found him 'much improved'. He had bought jewellery and other presents for Alix in Paris, and he was anxious to get married. Queen Victoria decided to vet her future daughter-in-law before Bertie proposed. On her way to Germany to visit the Prince Consort's childhood haunts, she stayed briefly in Belgium and a meeting was arranged with Alix.

Though only seventeen, the Danish princess managed this interview with the aplomb of an experienced diplomat. In deference to the Queen's loss, she wore a simple black dress without jewellery; her hair was pulled back off her forehead. The Queen was most impressed. 'Alexandra is lovely, such a beautiful, refined profile, and quiet ladylike manner.'[20] She had satisfactory talks with Alix's parents, too, before continuing her journey.

Bertie arrived in Belgium hard on his mother's heels, determined to propose. On 9 September he confided in a letter to his mother: 'The all-important event has taken place today. I proposed to the Princess at Laeken and she accepted me; and I cannot tell you *how* grateful I am for it ... After a few commonplace remarks, Alexandra said you had given her the white heather. I said I hoped it would bring her good luck. I asked her how she liked our country, and if she would come some day to England, and how long she would remain. She said she hoped some time. I said that I hoped she would remain always there and then offered her my hand and my heart. She immediately said *Yes*. I then kissed her hand and she kissed me.'[21]

Bertie and Alix spent a few precious days in each other's company – under strict orders from Victoria that they were not to see each other alone unless 'in a room next to the Princess's mother's with the door open.'[22] They found they had a lot in common – both were more sporting than clever, both of them loved to dance and play practical jokes, and they were both eager to marry. The Princess had hooked the most eligible (and probably most handsome) bachelor in Europe; Bertie had acquired an exquisite bride. He wrote to Victoria: 'I frankly avow to you that I did not think it possible to love a person as I do her. She is so kind and good, and I feel sure will make my life a happy one. I only trust that God will give me strength to do the same for her.'[23]

After the engagement had been announced, Queen Victoria insisted that Alix should spend some time alone with her in England, while Bertie went on a cruise in the Mediterranean. The lovers were most unhappy at this idea, which meant a long separation. Alix dreaded the prospect of a gloomy time shut up with her future mother-in-law and complained to Bertie that she was being put 'on approval'. For his part, Bertie did not want to celebrate his coming-of-age at sea. However, the Queen would not change her mind; she was determined to use this opportunity to educate Alix in her future duties, and to 'Germanise' her ideas. The latter part of the plan failed. Alix remained determinedly loyal to Denmark and England, and anti-German, all her life, but the visit served a valuable purpose in establishing deep ties of affection between mother and daughter-in-law.

Alix brought a ray of sunshine to the Queen's sad life, and when she left Osborne, on 28 November, the Queen wrote to Vicky: 'Dear sweet Alix left us yesterday evening and I hardly could bear to let her go! I always tremble lest something should happen to her! She seems to be too charming. She loves us all, and was much affected when she left us.'[24] Bertie's brothers and sisters loved Alix as much as his mother did.

The winter months passed in a whirl of preparations for the wedding on 10 March. Queen Victoria found these most upsetting as they reminded her of her own wedding and her beloved Albert. She dealt with the questions of guest lists, protocol, arrangements for VIPs and so on reluctantly. The one bright spot on the horizon was that her elder daughter would come from Prussia to support her at the wedding. On 22 January the Queen wrote to Vicky: 'I shall not be able to send you the yacht as she will be wanted so soon after for Alix – but you shall have a packet either at Calais or wherever you like. I can I grieve to say not ask you to bring any of the dear children as we shall not have a hole to spare, and I must put the governesses even into the nursery. I have had to ask all the court attendants of Alix and two of her uncles and this . . . makes a fearful squeeze.'[25]

From money that his father had wisely invested, Bertie inherited a capital sum of around £600,000. Out of this he bought Sandringham House, in Norfolk. This rambling country house, which needed extensive alterations, was to become the Prince and Princess of Wales's real home – Alix spent most of her later married life there, and eventually died in the house when she was nearly eighty.

'Bertie returns today – and then my bad headaches will begin I fear,' wrote Queen Victoria, on 28 January, 'but he is very much pleased with his place [Sandringham] and takes great interest in it.'[26] She wrote again to Vicky on 4 February, a real lament: 'Oh! If it only was all over! I dread the whole thing awfully and wonder even how you can rejoice so much at witnessing what must I should think be to you, who loved Papa so dearly, so terribly sad a wedding!'[27]

Unlike their Queen, the people of England were determined to celebrate the wedding in style. London planned a five-day festival leading up to the wedding, ending with a 'general illumination' on the wedding night. For a week previously, all the gas companies saved up – private houses were put on half ration, and street lamps not lit until long after their usual time. Great celebrations were planned in all parts of the country.

Alix and her parents left Copenhagen on 26 February. They travelled in style, fêted all the way, through Cologne and Brussels to Antwerp, where they boarded the royal yacht *Victoria and Albert* for the last stage of their journey to England.

An excited Bertie met the boat at Gravesend, and delighted the crowds by springing aboard and kissing Alix in public. The royal couple and their entourage went by special train to London, cheered all the way, where they transferred to six open carriages.

Alix travelled in a light grey dress and violet jacket with sable trimmings, and a white bonnet covered with red rosebuds that she had stitched herself. The crowds roared their appreciation of the Danish princess's beauty, and threatened to overturn the carriages in their enthusiasm to get near her. Outside the Mansion House, the Life Guards had to draw their sabres and breast a way through the people, but Alix continued to smile calmly.

It was dark and pouring with rain by the time the party reached Windsor Castle. Victoria greeted them in the hall, and kissed Alix warmly but was too overcome to dine with her guests. That night she recorded in her journal that, before dinner, 'Alix knocked at the door, peeped in and came and knelt before me with that sweet loving expression which spoke volumes. I was much moved and kissed her again and again.'[28]

The day before the wedding, the Queen took Bertie and Alix to see Albert's mausoleum at Frogmore. She joined their hands in front of his great tomb, and embraced them both, saying '*He* gives you his blessing.'[29]

The 10th of March 1863 dawned 'somewhat dull and chill', according to the *Illustrated London News*, 'but in a short time the sun shone bright and warm'. St George's Chapel, Windsor, was full to bursting with guests: the men in uniforms and plumes, trains, robes of the Garter with stars, rivières of diamonds, and some with their coat seams embroidered with gold lace; the women in colourful dresses 'three yards long, and some with ostrich feathers on their heads'.

In contrast, Queen Victoria wore black widow's weeds and 'a widow's cap more hideous than any I have yet seen',[30] wrote one of the guests afterwards. Her only ornaments were the star and ribbon of the Garter, and a miniature of the Prince Consort. She sat with her ladies-in-waiting (also wearing black) in Catherine of Aragon's pew – 'a high closet placed over the north side of the communion table and hung with drapery of purple and gold'.[31]

Below her, before the altar, her son waited for his bride. Bertie wore the uniform of a general, with a high gold collar, under the flowing purple robes of the Garter. 'He looked very like a gentleman and more *considerable* than he is wont to do,'[32] noted an eyewitness. Several times before the bride arrived he glanced nervously around the congregation and up at his mother.

Alix had been given a beautiful dress, made from Brussels lace, by King Leopold, but she was not allowed to wear it since it was deemed too unpatriotic. Instead, she wore a dress made of silver-tissue, trimmed with Honiton lace in an ornate pattern, and the skirt garlanded with loops of orange blossom. Bertie had given her £15,000 worth of jewellery, and she put a necklace of diamonds and pearls around her slim neck. Her long train was carried by eight unmarried daughters of earls and countesses, all in white.

Her great beauty was admired by all the guests, and Lord Clarendon wrote afterwards that he had never seen in anyone 'more grace and dignity and aplomb. Her eyes and the tip of her nose were a tiny bit red and accounted for by her having cried all the morning at leaving her mother, for ever, as she must feel. She said to one of the Princesses "you perhaps think I like marrying your Brother for his position but if he was a cowboy I should love him just the same and would marry no one else".' [33]

Jenny Lind led the singing of the choir, and when they sang a chorale composed by the late Prince Consort many of the congregation (especially Queen Victoria and her daughters) were moved to tears.

Lord Granville closed his account of the wedding with the words: 'the music good – the service not too long . . . rather a scramble for luncheon'.[34] 'Luncheon' was a sumptuous wedding breakfast attended by the bride and groom and thirty-six other Royals, though poor Queen Victoria did not feel up to it. At 4 o'clock the bride and groom left to honeymoon at Osborne on the Isle of Wight. That evening, the Queen wrote in her Journal that the honeymoon carriage had stopped beneath her window and she had seen 'Bertie standing up and both of them looking up lovingly at me'.[35]

Vicky and her husband, Fritz, went to see the honeymooners at Osborne, and Vicky wrote to her mother: 'It does one good to see people so thoroughly happy as this dear young couple are. As for Bertie, he looks blissful . . . Darling Alix looks charming and lovely and they both seem so comfortable and at home together.'[36]

Lord Alfred Tennyson, poet laureate of the day, composed a verse to commemorate the wedding, which began:

> Sea King's daughter from over the sea
> Alexandra!
> Saxon and Norman and Dane are we,

But all of us Dane in our welcome of thee,
Alexandra.

Some time later, when the poet met the Princess for the first time, she asked him to read the verse to her, and they both collapsed on the floor in fits of giggles. However, it was an accurate reflection of the way in which the English – from monarch to labourer – took the young bride to their hearts.

The Prince and Princess of Wales spent the early years of their married life in a constant whirl of social activities, and they injected a sense of gaiety into public life that had been lacking since Prince Albert's death. More and more during her long reign, Queen Victoria was to withdraw from the world, and though she worried that her son's life was 'too frivolous', in fact Bertie and Alix did much good in keeping the spirit of monarchy in the forefront of people's minds.

Alix's first child and the next heir to the throne – poor, ill-fated Eddy – was born prematurely, less than two years after the wedding. Alix produced four more children: she was a loving and devoted mother, and concentrated her life increasingly round her children at Sandringham as she grew older. Bertie never lost his eye for a pretty girl and had many affairs during their marriage, but he had a deep affection for his wife. He tolerated her deafness and unpunctuality, only once losing patience when he strode into her bedroom before their coronation remarking: 'My dear Alix, if you don't come immediately you won't be crowned Queen.'[37] For her part Alix tolerated Bertie's affairs, forever turning a blind eye and taking her husband's part in any scandals. She showed her particular generosity of spirit when Bertie, aged sixty-eight and now King, was dying. Alix sent for his mistress of long standing, Mrs Keppel, to give her the opportunity to say goodbye.

CHAPTER THREE

GEORGIE AND PRINCESS MAY

On a June day in 1867, Queen Victoria set out for her childhood home – Kensington Palace – to see the baby girl born to her first cousin, the ample Princess Mary Adelaide of Cambridge. The Queen, who had agreed to be the baby's godmother, bent over the cradle and pronounced the infant 'a very fine child'. Fate had begun to weave one of its more intricate patterns round the figures assembled in the lofty bedroom. By an odd coincidence, the baby had been born in the same apartments and almost on the same day as Queen Victoria, and that small stout figure was to loom over her life like a benevolent fairy godmother. Years later, the Queen was to write to Princess May: 'I like to feel your birthday is so near to mine, that you were born in the same House as I was & that you bear my name.'[1]

The baby, christened Victoria Mary Augusta Louise Olga Pauline Claudine Agnes, and known to her family as May, was to be the only girl in a family of four. Her mother, the daughter of the Duke of Cambridge and a granddaughter of George III, was enormously fat, warm-hearted and with a total disregard for time and money from which her whole family were to suffer in later years. But she was genuinely compassionate, deeply involved in charitable works, and was a great favourite with the British people who enjoyed her extrovert nature.

Her size had inhibited suitors, and she eventually married in her middle thirties, a man four years younger than herself. His Serene Highness, Prince Franz of Teck was the son of Duke Alexander of Württemberg; strikingly good looking, he was prevented by his father's morganatic marriage from marrying into the hidebound German courts.

Queen Victoria, ever susceptible to male beauty, was much struck by the Prince's dark good looks and wrote to her daughter the Crown Princess of Prussia: 'I do wish one cld find some more black eyed Pces or Pcesses for *our* children! ... For that constant fair hair & blue eyes makes the blood so lymphatic – Dear Alix has added *no* strength to the family ... darling Papa *often* with vehemence said: *"We must have some strong dark blood"*.[2]

Perhaps as a result of all that rich dark blood, Princess May grew up a strong and sturdy little girl – though perversely fair-haired and blue-eyed – studious, sensible and serious-minded. Princess Mary Adelaide may not have known how to handle money, but she did know how to bring up children, with affection tempered by a healthy dose of discipline, and personally super-vised their education.

May's happy, industrious childhood days, divided between Kensington Palace and White Lodge, her parents' 'country' home in Richmond Park, were in sharp contrast to the way the children of the Prince of Wales were growing up in the splendours of Marlborough House.

Alexandra, the beautiful Princess of Wales, a cousin of Princess Mary Adelaide, was a doting and over-indulgent mother. The children under her care lacked discipline and any sense of purpose, and even as a child May found their games and occupations juvenile. But Alexandra and Mary Adelaide were close friends and the two families saw a great deal of one another, at Sandringham, White Lodge and Marlborough House. 'Today is Georgie's birth-day, can your little girl come and play with them after luncheon?'[3] Alexandra wrote to her cousin Mary on 3 June 1870, litttle dream-ing that the fair-haired toddler would one day become her daughter-in-law in dramatic circumstances.

When Princess May was sixteen, her mother's extravagance fin-ally caught up with her. Pressed by creditors and her own family, the Tecks left White Lodge to spend some time on the Continent, hopefully living quietly and inexpensively. They spent most of the next two years in a borrowed villa outside Florence, and it was per-haps here, amid the glories of Renaissance Italy, in the mellow sunshine, that the Princess's life-long interest in beautiful things was born.

A tall girl, with golden brown hair, piercing blue eyes and the upright carriage she was to keep all her life, May visited museums and art galleries, spent warm afternoons sketching in the sunshine.

This two-year 'exile' and her work for her mother's endless charities brought the Princess into contact with aspects of life that someone in her position might not have been aware of and gave her a healthy respect for the value of money.

In 1885, the Tecks moved back to White Lodge, and for the next six years Princess May acted as her mother's secretary and companion, helping with her charities, reading and studying. James Pope-Hennessy, in his perceptive biography, describes her at this period of her life as 'a silent, slim fair girl in that epoch of the hour-glass figure, the bustle, the minute bonnet, the poodle hairstyle and the muff.'[4] Very shy, she was ill at ease amid the brittle small talk of London parties and dances.

Although she was of royal blood, her father's morganatic blood put her in an anomalous position – too royal for an ordinary marriage, not quite royal enough to find a suitor among the mass of German princelings who had provided husbands for so many of Queen Victoria's daughters.

In 1886 her grandmother, the old Duchess of Cambridge, had suggested a match between May and the Russian Grand Duke Michael Michailovitch, grandson of Czar Nicholas I. But the Princess's father had refused to see his only daughter exiled to Russia and regarded Russian Grand Dukes as poor matrimonial risks. So the young Princess spent her days quietly at White Lodge, serene and apparently contented, her fair head bent over her books, a young woman of twenty-four, 'with a soul above buttons,'[5] in the happy phrase of a certain Miss Ella Taylor writing to her sister from White Lodge.

The scene at Marlborough House was less idyllic. The eldest son of the Prince of Wales, heir presumptive to the British throne, was His Royal Highness, Prince Albert Victor, Duke of Clarence and Avondale. 'Eddy' to his family and nicknamed 'Collars-and-Cuffs' by his father because he wore a high starched collar to hide his very long neck, was a slightly-built young man with a poor constitution, few interests and a total lack of application to anything save self-indulgence. Weak from birth – he was born prematurely in January 1864 – he joined the Navy as a cadet with his younger brother Georgie, but failed to benefit from the open-air life, the round-the-world travel or the rigorous discipline. Eddy had inherited little of his mother's beauty, but a good deal of both his parents' considerable charm, and the charm worked, particularly with the ladies; by his mid-twenties Eddy had been in and out of love several times.

'A good sensible wife – with considerable character – is what he needs most,' the Prince of Wales wrote to his mother, Queen Victoria, who was alarmed by the tales of the Prince's dissipated life, 'but where is she to be found?'[6] In an attempt to find her for himself, Eddy fancied himself deeply in love with his beautiful cousin Alix of Hesse. But Alix turned him down, only to become the ill-fated last Czarina of Russia.

Next came an infatuation with Hélène, the pretty daughter of the Comte de Paris. Hélène was a Catholic, but prepared to give up her religion, and Queen Victoria, whose heart was always touched by romance, was sympathetic to the young couple. Not so the Comte de Paris, who was horrified at the thought of his daughter's apostasy. Hélène's personal plea to the Pope failed, and the match came to nothing.

The search for the good and sensible wife was beginning to narrow nearer home, to the quiet princess at White Lodge. In November 1891 came a significant summons – an invitation for Princess May and her eldest brother, Adolphus, known as 'Dolly', to spend ten days at Balmoral with her godmother the Queen. It was the first wave of the royal wand.

'Your dear Children arrived safely after 12, looking very well,'[7] the Queen telegraphed to Princess Mary Adelaide on their arrival. The visit was a great success and laid the foundations for the mutual respect and affection which were to mark the relations between the two remarkable women. Victoria wrote to her daughter the Empress Frederick of Prussia: 'We have seen a gt. deal of May & Dolly Teck during these last 10 days . . . & I cannot say enough good of them. May is a particularly nice girl, so quiet & yet cheerful & so very carefully brought up & so sensible . . . I think & hope that Eddy will try & marry her for I think she is a superior girl.'[8] Queen Victoria had no prejudices about morganatic marriages, luckily for her grandchildren.

Eddy duly proposed to his cousin May – sooner than either his parents or his grandmother had anticipated – at a county ball at Luton Hoo, at that time the home of the Danish ambassador. The entry in Princess May's diary for 3 December 1891 reads: 'To my great surprise Eddy proposed to me during the evening in Mme de Falbe's boudoir – Of course I said yes – We are both very happy – Kept it secret from everybody but Mama & Papa.'[9] The engagement was announced to the nation on 7 December, and the Princess travelling back to London had her first taste of a royal welcome from the cheering crowd waiting for her at the railway station.

Queen Victoria was delighted. 'God bless them both!' she wrote in her Journal. 'I'm so thankful, as I had much wished for this marriage, thinking her so suitable.'[10] She wasn't alone in her high opinion of the young princess. Her grandson, Willy, the German Emperor, wrote to the Queen on a cosy note of family gossip: 'What happy and interesting news! Eddy is engaged! . . . He is indeed a lucky creature and may look forward to a happy life! For a handsomer and more accomplished young Princess is rarely to be found.'[11]

The wedding was fixed for 27 February, and the Queen promised the couple apartments in St James's Palace. She wrote to May: 'Let me . . . say *how much* I rejoice at your becoming my grandchild & how much confidence I have in you, to fill worthily the important position to which you are called by your marriage with Eddy.'[12]

The wedding preparations went ahead as December slipped into a bitterly cold January, bringing a particularly virulent form of influenza. Early in the new year Princess May and her parents joined the Prince of Wales's family at Sandringham. It was to be a festive gathering to celebrate Eddy's twenty-eighth birthday on 8 January; it ended tragically with the Prince's death, after only a week's illness. What started as a cold turned to influenza, pneumonia set in and Eddy died after hours of delirium in the presence of his helpless family and his stricken bride-to-be.

The suddenness of the tragedy, and its cruel timing, shocked the country. The old Queen, who had endured so much personal tragedy in her life felt the blow keenly both as grandmother and as monarch.

'14th January – A never-to-be-forgotten day!' her faithful Journal records. 'Whilst I was dressing, Lenchen [her daughter Princess

Helena] came in, bringing the following heart-rending telegram from poor Bertie: "Our darling Eddy has been taken from us. We are broken-hearted." Words are far too poor to express one's feelings of grief, horror and distress! Poor, poor parents; poor May, to have her whole bright future to be merely a dream! Poor me, in my old age to see this young promising life cut short!'[13]

'We always say God's Will be done,' the Prince of Wales wrote to his mother, 'and it is right to say and think so, but it does seem hard to rob us of our eldest son, on the eve of his marriage ... and ... that poor little May should virtually become a widow before she is a wife.'[14]

The Duke of Clarence was buried on 20 January. Among the family flowers, the most personal and touching tribute was from his fiancée – May's bridal wreath of orange blossom, placed on his coffin. From Sandringham Princess Mary Adelaide wrote to the Queen who had been advised by her doctors not to make the sad journey in the bitter weather. 'He lies amid flowers, chiefly *Maiblumen – Her* flower *now* being *woven* for the wedding train!'[15]

Princess Mary was piling on the agony, but May's position was indeed deserving of pity, as she returned to White Lodge, a pale, subdued figure in strict mourning, the bright dream of a royal wedding fading like a mirage before the grim reality of the grey London winter. Perhaps the most affected by the tragedy was the new heir presumptive, twenty-six-year-old Prince George, recovering from a serious attack of typhoid fever and shattered by the death of the brother he had been close to and loved dearly.

Unlike his brother, George Frederick Ernest Albert ('Georgie' to his family) had sterling qualities. Smaller than Eddy, but sturdily built, he had a distinctly Naval air with his bright blue eyes, golden brown hair, beard and moustaches. He was devoted to his lovely mother, 'Darling Motherdear', loved the Navy and was deeply attached to Sandringham, the home of his childhood holidays.

Shy and diffident, he now found himself in the invidious position of being in direct line to a throne he had not been prepared to ascend, and under strong pressure to get married. His father warned him that Queen Victoria was 'in a terrible fuss' about his marrying. Actually, she had been fussing since February 1891, but the young prince, in a typically forthright letter, had set her right: 'I quite agree with you Dearest Grandmama, & understand your reasons for wishing Eddy & I to marry as soon as possible. But still I think marrying too young is a bad thing . . . the one thing I never could do is to marry a person that didn't care for me . . . I should be miserable for the rest of my life.'[16]

But life, in its roundabout way, had paved the way for him to marry a woman of exceptional quality, ideally suited to him personally, and one who would help and support him in all the trials of his position. None the less, there were difficult days ahead for the young couple. It was obvious that everyone, from Queen Victoria to the Teck family, ardently wished that George would marry May.

It was an awkward situation for the sensitive princess, and to ease matters and give the pale, sad girl a change, Princess Mary took her family to the South of France in early spring. Her choice of holiday spot was not fortuitous: the Prince of Wales was due to visit Cap Martin with his family. And, as Princess Mary had foreseen, Georgie called on his cousin soon after arriving and the young people, brought together by their grief, saw a great deal of one another.

Back in England, Princess May spent the anniversary of her engagement with the family of the Prince of Wales at Sandringham, where, in truly Victorian fashion, Eddy's room was kept as a shrine – with a fire burning in the grate, flowers in the vases and a Union Jack draping the bed. May was very touched to be given a beautiful rivière of diamonds – it was to have been her in-laws' wedding present – and a fitted case which Eddy had chosen for her.

In this loaded emotional atmosphere, the uneasy courtship of George and May progressed slowly and painfully. In March 1893 Alexandra took her son away on a cruise to Greece. During this time May and Georgie exchanged shy, rather stilted letters. Here is one from the Prince: 'You say that I will think your letter dull, on the contrary . . . it interested me very much, if half the people who write letters, wrote as well as you it would be a blessing . . . I hope [this letter] won't bore you too much, when you are stop & throw it away.'[17]

May and Georgie were too well schooled in royal traditions and too aware of their responsibilities to the British throne not to do what was expected of them, and on 3 May 1893 Princess May accepted her second royal proposal in eighteen months, in the garden of Sheen Lodge, the home of Georgie's sister, the Duchess of Fife.

Immediately Queen Victoria wrote to the Prince. 'Let me now say how thankful I am that this great and so long & ardently-wished-for event is settled.' The old Queen was shrewd and perceptive, and added: 'Say everything affectionate to Dear May, for whom this must be a trying moment *full of such mixed feelings*. But she cannot find a *better* husband than you, and I am sure she will be a good, devoted and useful wife to you.'[18]

Alexandra's reaction was less whole-hearted. From Malta she cabled her son: 'With what mixed feeling I read your telegram! Well, all I can say is that I pray God to give you both a long and happy life together and you will make up for Dear May all that she lost in Darling Eddy, and that you will be a mutual happiness to each other, a comfort to us, and a blessing to the nation.'[19]

To May she wrote: 'Let me welcome you back once more as my dear daughter . . . you know *how* much I have always loved you – & how glad I am that you will still belong to us . . . and I hope that my sweet May will always come straight to me for everything . . . Ever yr most loving & devoted old Motherdear.'[20] Alexandra genuinely loved May, but she was a possessive mother who never realised that her children were grown up and she was to prove a trying mother-in-law.

Despite the somewhat anomalous circumstances, the engagement was popular with the nation which had shared in the Princess's bereavement and wanted to see her happy. *The Times*, in a rather gloomy editorial, expressed the wish 'that a union rooted in painful memories may prove happy beyond the common lot,' and the *London Sketch* published this extraordinary eulogy: 'Princess May is very practical and has an excellent head for organisation . . . She is not a fashionable young lady . . . she does not play tennis; she has never tried golf . . . she is not enthusiastic about riding, although she can ride gracefully, she does not talk slang . . . Princess May is not an advanced girl, she holds no great theories about the emancipation of women . . . her tastes are essentially womanly.' In fact, the future Queen of England was highly intelligent, with an intellectual curiosity which far outstripped the way of life of her in-laws.

The eight weeks of the engagement were a difficult time for the young couple whose nerves had been strained by the dramatic circumstances which had brought them together. The Princess wrote to her fiancé: 'This is a simply horrid time we are going through & I am only looking forward to the time when you & I shall be alone at Sandringham . . . I am very sorry that I am still so shy with you . . . I *love* you more than any body in the world, & this I cannot tell you myself, so I write it to relieve my feelings.'[21]

The preparations for the wedding on 6 July in the Chapel Royal of St James's Palace were going ahead, and the presents, valued at over £300,000, started to arrive. Among the most welcome was £1,000 from the Princess's aunt Augusta, Duchess of Mecklenburg-Strelitz, and her husband. It paid for the Princess's second trousseau which would have stretched the family's always precarious finances.

On the day before the wedding, the Princess called on Queen Victoria to receive her gifts, 'the Victoria and Albert Order, a handsome diamond necklace, stuffs and shawls, Indian and others, and a fine flounce of old lace, which had belonged to Queen Charlotte, with all of which May seemed much pleased.'[22]

There were four gigantic bridal cakes, adding up to a mountain of rich fruit, marzipan and sugar. One cake was made by Mr Searcy for the garden party given by the Duke and Duchess of Teck in honour of their daughter's marriage. At the wedding itself there was the cake ordered by the Prince and Princess of Wales, in three tiers, each supported by pillars, standing on a silver stand. Messrs Gunter & Co made a cake specially for the occasion, which measured over 5ft in height, and the loyal ladies of Cheltenham presented a 7ft cake to the Princess. It was a gorgeous creation in four tiers, embellished with designs in silver and gold.

Like Queen Victoria, May wrote to her bridegroom on the morning of her wedding, and though the tone is less ecstatic, there is no doubt about the sincerity of the simple note. 'I should much like to give you a wedding ring if you will wear it for my sake – I therefore send you herewith one or two to try on for size – Let me have the one you choose at once & I will give it to you in the chapel.

What a memorable day in our lives this will be. God grant it may bring us much happiness, I love you with all my heart. Yrs for ever & ever – May.'[23]

The 6th of July was a summer's day of unequalled beauty. The streets of London were bright with decorations, St James's converted into a bower with festoons of leaves and the white roses of York.

'Lovely women continued to hurry down St James's Street on their daintily slippered feet, showing a deal of silk stockings,' wrote the correspondent of *The Queen, the Lady's Newspaper*, adding that 'the beauty of the dresses and the magnificence of the jewels baffle description and those worn by the Indian Princes now in London were very remarkable.'

We are told by the same indefatigable journalist that 'HRH the Princess May of Teck intrusted the arrangement of her hair and veil . . . to M. Dupont . . . who has often dressed her hair before.' The veil, of fine old Honiton point, had been worn by her mother at her own wedding. 'The fringe was lightly curled upon her forehead and placed rather forward was a coronet of orange blossom. The rest of the fringe behind was a little raised to fill the space between this and a magnificent diamond tiara.'

The bridal bouquet was of rare white flowers, with the old Provence rose 'House of York' predominating, and included white orchids, lilies of the valley, orange blossom and a new white carnation called 'The Bride'. The ten bridesmaids wore white satin dresses trimmed with silver lace.

'Princess May is an ideal bride,' enthused the correspondent of the *Lady's Newspaper*, 'and has bravely borne the tremendous ordeal of a long progress through the streets of London.' But for the most vivid account of the day let us turn to that natural reporter, Queen Victoria, who by some error of timing arrived at the Chapel before the guests, instead of last as protocol dictated. She refused all suggestions that she should retire to some nearby room and thoroughly enjoyed seeing all the guests arriving. She left this record of the wedding in her Journal. 'The great day, so anxiously looked forward, was very bright and fine, but overpoweringly hot . . . I wore my wedding lace over a light black stuff and my wedding veil surmounted by a small coronet. While I was dressing, Mary brought in May who looked very sweet. Her dress was very simple, of white satin, with a silver design of roses, shamrocks, thistles and orange flowers interwoven. On her hair, she had a small wreath of orange flowers, myrtle and white heather, surmounted by the diamond necklace I gave her, which can also be worn as a diadem.'[24] The ten bridesmaids, mostly cousins, included little Alice Battenberg, later to become the mother of the Duke of Edinburgh. The Queen's Journal continues: 'Georgie gave his answers very distinctly, while May though quite self-possessed, spoke very low . . . I could not but remember that I had stood where May did fifty three years ago . . . may these dear children's happiness last longer! . . . After the last hymn and the benediction, they came forward to kiss my hand, and I embraced them affectionately . . . We got home before anyone else . . . went to the middle room, with the balcony, over-looking the Mall, and stepped out amidst much cheering. Very soon the Bride and Bridegroom arrived and I stepped out on the balcony with them, taking her by the hand, which produced another great outburst of cheering.'[25]

How many times this scene was to be repeated over the years as royal bride after royal bride stepped out on the balcony of Buckingham Palace to wave shyly at the crowd in the middle of her newly acquired family!

The Queen continues: 'We got rather late to luncheon, which was served in the large dining-room.'[26] This was the State Dining Room, where eight tables, each laid for eight guests with the Queen in the centre, provided the setting for the family and intimate friends. In the Great Ball Room of the Palace a buffet was laid for 250 guests.

Later the Queen writes how she went to her room 'to see the young couple go away . . . Dear May came in looking very pretty in a dress of white poplin, edged with gold, and a pretty little toque with roses.'[27]

Queen Victoria's sharp eyes may have been misted with emotion, because the Princess's going-away hat is described by that other Queen, the Lady's Newspaper, as 'a gold bonnet with a cluster of cream plumes.' She wore a cape 'with a deep frill of rich Irish lace down the front and round the collar . . . held to the figure at the waist with cream satin ribbon.'

Later that evening, the honeymoon couple arrived at York Cottage on the Sandringham estate, covered in dust from the country road leading from Wolferton to Sandringham. York Cottage, the Prince of Wales's gift to his son, was a gloomy little structure. Originally built to house the overflow of guests from the big house, it was as unpretentious as a suburban villa, but it was to remain Georgie's favourite home. The Princess found that the whole house had been furnished by her bridegroom, mostly from Maples.

The honeymoon was not an ideal time for the couple. The weather, after the glorious wedding day, turned wet and dreary; they were both still very shy and ill at ease with each other, and spent their days quietly, going for drives, playing cards and reading to each other. After less than two weeks, the whole Wales family arrived at the big house, and the young people's privacy was ended. Alexandra and her daughters would drop in on the couple – even at breakfast – and there were constant invitations to lunch and dinner. But despite all this, during those July days in Norfolk, Georgie fell in love with his bride. He was to write to her: 'When I asked you to marry me, I was very fond of you, but not very much in love with you, but I saw in *you* the person I was capable of loving most deeply, if you only returned that love ... I know now that I do *love* you darling girl with all my *heart* & am simply *devoted* to you ... I *adore you sweet May*, I can't say more than that.'[28]

Queen Victoria had been right in assessing May's character and the more she saw of her the more she grew to like and admire her. She wrote to her eldest daughter in Prussia: 'She strikes me more and more as vy clever & so sensible & right minded & is a great help to Georgie.'

When George came to the throne on the death of his father in 1910 he wrote in the diary he kept all his life: 'I have lost my best friend & the best of fathers ... but God will help me in my great responsibilities & darling May will be my comfort as she always has been.'[29]

This she was to be through forty-two years of married life and a reign which included the bloodiest of world wars. As the pretty girl grew into a handsome woman and a stately old lady, she never lost her Edwardian image; her hairstyle, her clothes stayed the same.

With her famous toques, her parasols, her erect carriage, she was a truly well-loved figure, every inch a queen, the very symbol of royalty to the British people and to her family.

CHAPTER FOUR

ELIZABETH AND THE DUKE OF YORK

From about 7 am on Thursday, 26 April 1923, under a damp spring sky that promised further bouts of rain, a knot of people began to gather outside No 17 Bruton Street. They were waiting to see the bride. Inside her London home, Lady Elizabeth Bowes-Lyon spent her last morning as a commoner happily – with her parents the Earl and Countess of Strathmore, her beloved brother David and other members of her closely-knit Scottish family. There was a certain amount of commotion of the kind generally associated with weddings . . .

Two miles away, the bridegroom's family were also preparing for the wedding, to the sound of good-humoured cheers from the crowds that pressed shoulder to shoulder round Queen Victoria's statue and the gates of Buckingham Palace. For the groom, there was a ceremony to attend before his wedding – when his father, King George V, conferred upon him the ancient Order of the Thistle. This honour was intended as a compliment to Lady Elizabeth's Scottish origins.

The young groom wore the uniform of a group captain in the Royal Air Force, with the Garter Riband and Star, the Order of the Thistle, gold aiguillettes over his right shoulder, and a single row of medals including his service decorations from the First World War. He was a fine, straight figure in his blue uniform, with clean-cut good looks, eyes well set apart and a sensitive mouth. Bertie – as his family called him – did not specially resemble either parent but had a look of them both, according to Queen Marie of Roumania who had written the year before to George: 'Somehow your boy in some ways reminds me so much of you, though he has exactly May's smile.'[1]

At 11.08 precisely King George V, resplendent in his uniform of Admiral of the Fleet, accompanied by Queen Mary 'magnificently regal in an aquamarine-blue and silver dress with lace overdress embroidered with blue crystals on the corsage and skirt and glorious diamonds',[2] drove out of Buckingham Palace. They were flanked by the great horses of the Sovereign's Escort of Household Cavalry.

Four minutes later, Lady Elizabeth, wearing an ivory coloured dress of fine chiffon moire in a simple medieval style, under a beautiful *Point de Flandres* shawl lent to her by Queen Mary, left 17 Bruton Street with her father. They travelled to the Abbey in a state landau, but with just four metropolitan police as their escort, since the bride was still a commoner. Lady Elizabeth looked calm and happy; she waved to the crowds with delight, and chatted to cheer up her father who seemed quite cast down at the prospect of 'losing' his daughter.

Inside Westminster Abbey, 3,000 guests waited. There were the groom's grandmother, Queen Alexandra, now eighty-two, but as good-looking as ever in a violet and gold outfit; her sister, Her Imperial Majesty the Empress Marie Dagmar of Russia; and many more crowned heads from all over the world including five Indian princes who were staying at the Savoy. There were also leading politicians, and the cream of the English aristocracy. *The Times* of the day recorded the following famous figures present in the Abbey: 'Lord and Lady Carson, Mr. Lloyd George, Mr. Asquith in Trinity House Uniform, Mrs. Asquith with an almond green marocain wrap drawn tightly round her ... the Duchess of Rutland in a ruby cloak, Lady Diana Duff Cooper, Mr. Ramsay MacDonald ... Everywhere one noticed that feathers were worn more than flowers; paradise and trailing shaded ostrich mounts were to be seen on large and small hats, of which there were about equal numbers ... One of the last of the great ladies was the Marchioness of Lansdowne in pearl-grey embroidered in cut steel ... she wore the badges of the Royal Order of Victoria and Albert, the Imperial Order of the Crown of India, the Companion of Honour, that of Lady Justice of the Order of St. John of Jerusalem in England and the ribbon and star of the Order of the British Empire. Lady Lansdowne wore pearl and diamond ornaments but the puzzle must have been to get all the badges on the left side of her bodice.'

Soon after the King and Queen had taken their seats opposite the bride's family, the groom arrived with his elder brother, Ed-

54

ward, Prince of Wales, and young Prince George. Edward, heir to the throne and a year older than Bertie, was the best man; he wore the dashing red uniform of the Grenadier Guards, while Prince George – later Duke of Kent – wore the colours of the 10th Hussars. The sight of her three good-looking grandsons, with their fair hair and dazzling uniforms, proved too much for the Dowager Queen Alix who slipped from her pew on an impulse to hug each of them in turn.

At exactly 11.30, the bride arrived. It was the moment the crowds round the Abbey and the guests inside had been awaiting. And for the bridegroom, looking nervous but happy, it signified the end of a long courtship.

Bertie and Lady Elizabeth first met – according to her father – when she was about five. They went to the same children's party, and Lady Elizabeth – whose manners were already impeccable – offered Bertie the crystallised cherries off her piece of cake. He was only nine, but she obviously made a lasting impression for he recognised her at once the next time he saw her, thirteen years later.

Elizabeth was a graceful and engaging child, with long dark hair, deep blue eyes and a lovely smile. She had natural composure. In his excellent book *Thirty Years a Queen*, Geoffrey Wakeford tells the following anecdote of Lady Elizabeth, who, when barely five, greeted her father's factor, Mr. Ralston: 'How do you do, Mr. Ralston?' And then volunteered the information: 'I haven't seen you look so well, not for years and years, and I'm sure you'll be sorry to know that Lord Strathmore has got the tooth-ache.'[3] Other visitors to the Bowes-Lyon household remember being greeted by a smiling Elizabeth with the inviting words: 'Shall us sit and talk?'

In contrast to Elizabeth's self-confidence, Bertie was a highly-strung, shy child. His parents loved him dearly, but were quite strict, as this letter from his father shows: 'Now that you are five years old I hope you will always try and be obedient and do at once what you are told, as you will find it will come much easier to you the sooner you begin.'[4]

Bertie's grandparents, the old King Edward VII and Queen Alix, delighted in spoiling their grandchildren – but at home in York Cottage the children were made to practise self-control. At seven, Bertie developed a stammer which may have been partly due to his nervous temperament and to the fact that though naturally left-handed he was forced to do things with his right hand. He had another physical problem: knock-knees. And to cure this the doctors devised a series of most uncomfortable splints which he had to wear at certain hours of the day and night. It must have seemed to the boy that you had to suffer to be royal.

Like his brothers, Bertie was educated at home until the age of thirteen, when his father sent him to naval college at Osborne, with instructions that he was to be treated like any other cadet. In fact, despite his royal birth, Bertie was at a distinct disadvantage: he was 'shy and nervous and abnormally homesick, he had never played a serious game of cricket or football, had never sat in a class of more than three . . . Moreover his stammer incited the natural brutality inherent in small boys,'5 but the young prince had guts and his first letter home was a brave lie, 'I have quite settled down here now,'6 he wrote to his mother at the end of a week.

Osborne was followed by Dartmouth and a final training cruise on the 9,800-ton cruiser *Cumberland* in foreign waters before he was appointed (on 15 September 1913) to HMS *Collingwood*. Here Bertie took his turn at the unglamorous daily round of midshipman, and for practical purposes was known as 'Mr Johnson'.

He loved the Navy, and for the first time learned to relax with people and to make friends. He soon earned the liking and respect of his contemporaries and his teachers. Unlike his debonair elder brother, Edward, Bertie did not have a charismatic personality but he had qualities of genuine worth. 'He never shirked, never malingered, never gave up in a game or race or sport. He was generous and loyal, with an abundance of fun and mischief and one of his most pleasing traits was that he never talked "up" or "down".'7

This, then, was the young man who came back into Lady Elizabeth's life when she was in her late teens. The graceful child of five named Elizabeth after a Queen, Angela because she reminded her father of an angel, and Marguerite after the Moon Daisy, had grown into a beautiful young woman.

She had had a wonderful childhood. Her father owned three

houses: St Paul's Walden Bury in Hertfordshire where Elizabeth was born and subsequently got engaged; a house off Berkeley Square, London; and Glamis Castle. Glamis had belonged to the Bowes-Lyon family for over 500 years, since Princess Jean (daughter of Robert II) married Sir John Lyon. It is a fairy-tale castle surrounded by legend and superstitions and is believed to be the setting for Shakespeare's *Macbeth*. With its secret passages, trapdoors and concealed chambers in the sometimes 8ft-thick stone walls, it made a marvellous holiday home for the boisterous Bowes-Lyon children.

Lady Elizabeth and her brother David were the closest in the large family of ten – their parents referred to them as the 'two Benjamins', and they were inseparable. They worked and played together until the happy, relaxed family atmosphere was broken by the First World War. The Bowes-Lyons made Glamis Castle their main wartime residence, and opened it as a convalescent home to soldiers.

The eldest of the Bowes-Lyon sons went to war, with tragic results: Fergus, Elizabeth's elder brother, was killed at Loos, and Michael was taken prisoner, missing and believed dead for a long while. It was time to put away the games and grow up. Lady Elizabeth recorded: 'Lessons were neglected, for during those first few months we were so busy knitting, knitting, knitting and making shirts for the local battalion of the 5th Black Watch. My chief occupation was crumpling up tissue paper, until it was so soft that it no longer crackled, to put into the lining of sleeping bags.'[8]

Many of the soldiers who were looked after at Glamis took back with them to the front warm memories of the teenage girl who helped willingly to run the house and look after them. Sergeant Pearne later told Lady Cynthia Asquith: 'She had the loveliest pair of blue eyes I'd ever seen. Very expressive eloquent eyes that could speak for themselves. She had a very taking habit of knitting her forehead just a little now and then when speaking, and her smile was a refreshment.'[9]

Bertie, meanwhile, was on active service in the Navy. He saw war at first-hand, until severe gastric troubles invalided him out of ships and into the Royal Air Force. He became the first member of the Royal Family to hold a pilot's licence.

Lady Elizabeth was eighteen when the war ended, and she could enjoy a normal social life again. From then on, her time was divided between London and Scotland, with many quiet weekends spent in the peaceful gardens at St Paul's. She loved to dance, and was very good at it; she had many friends, and many admirers including the Duke of York. But for two years, the Earl's daughter held the King's son at arm's length. She was reluctant to commit herself; with quiet determination, Bertie persevered.

In the spring of 1921, the King and Queen came to stay at Glamis, and Queen Mary noted her second son's admiration for young Lady Elizabeth. Her friendly suspicions must have been further aroused when Bertie – staying for a second time with the Bowes-Lyons – wrote home saying 'It is delightful here and Elizabeth is very kind to me. The more I see of her the more I like her.'[10]

Early in 1922, Elizabeth was bridesmaid to Bertie's sister, Princess Mary, at a magnificent wedding in Westminster Abbey. (She is reported as looking lovely, though the official portrait painter made the mistake of leaving out his future Queen when painting some of the bridesmaids.) Increasingly, during 1922, the Duke of York visited the Bowes-Lyon household; and now the King and Queen were certain that he was in love. They approved whole-heartedly: even George V – usually so hard to please because he was a perfectionist – encouraged Bertie's suit, saying 'You'll be a lucky fellow if she accepts you.'[11]

One January weekend in 1923, Bertie plucked up courage to propose. Whilst Elizabeth's parents attended church with the other house guests, Bertie took Elizabeth for a walk in the beautiful woods surrounding St Paul's. That afternoon, overjoyed, he cabled his parents the pre-arranged signal: 'All right. Bertie.'[12] King George V recorded in his diary two days later: 'Bertie with Greig arrived after tea and informed us that he was engaged to Elizabeth Bowes-Lyon, to which we gladly gave our consent. I trust they will be very happy.'[13] The following weekend, Elizabeth and her parents were invited to Sandringham, and an approving Queen Mary noted: 'Elizabeth is charming, so pretty and engaging and natural. Bertie is supremely happy.'[14]

For the bride-to-be, life suddenly took on a different hue. For the first time, she experienced the glare of publicity that surrounds royalty, and she wrote to a friend: 'I feel very happy, but quite dazed. We hoped we were going to have a few days' peace first, but the cat is now completely out of the bag and there is no possibility of stuffing him back.'[15]

The wedding was arranged for April, and preparations began at once. For the first time since 1383 – when young King Richard II married 'Good Princess Anne of Bohemia' – it was decided that a prince of the royal blood should marry in Westminster Abbey.

The laborious process of drawing up a guest list of around 3,000 people began, and the wedding presents flooded in ... an ostrich feather mantelet, tied with ribbons, from South Africa; a thousand gold-eyed needles from the livery company of needle-makers; and many beautiful pieces of furniture, the item the young couple had expressed a preference for.

From her new family, Lady Elizabeth received jewellery. Bertie's engagement present was an oval sapphire ring from Kashmir set about with diamonds; he also gave her a necklace of pearls and diamonds with a matching pendant. The King gave her a tiara and complete set of diamonds and turquoises; from the Queen she received a sparkling diamond and sapphire necklace. Bertie's favourite present came from Elizabeth's mother – a miniature of the bride, framed in diamonds. He cherished this gift all his life.

For her wedding dress, Lady Elizabeth was careful to include an item that would help a depressed area of British industry – Nottingham lace, machine-made. She also instructed that this was to be used on her two train bearers' and six bridesmaids' dresses, as a trimming to the plain white georgette. Each bridesmaid wore a leaf-green tulle sash and her present from the bridegroom – a carved crystal brooch formed by the white rose of York, with a diamond centre of the initials E and A. Their bouquets were made up from white roses and heather. The bride wore a tulle veil, with a wreath of orange blossom and a white rose of York at each side. In the tradition of royal brides, the veil was pulled back from her face, revealing her lovely deep blue eyes and high cheek-bones, as she arrived at her wedding, on the stroke of 11.30.

Inside the Abbey, the train bearers and bridesmaids waited to take up their positions, and as the bride entered the sun came out, like an omen, flooding the building with a mellow light and sparkling on the gold aiguillettes of the groom waiting at the altar.

There was a slight delay in the proceedings, when one of the clergy fainted, and, whilst she waited for the procession to re-form, Lady Elizabeth suddenly left her father's side to place her own bouquet of white York Roses on the tomb of the Unknown Warrior, in a poignant tribute to her brother and so many friends lost in the First World War. Then, at her father's side, she moved forward to meet Bertie. 'The Duke of York faced with shining eyes and a look of happiness the girl who, hand in hand with her father, was advancing in her lovely old-fashioned dress, gleaming with silver and veiled in old lace ... they seemed to think of no one but each other,' wrote the reporter of *The Times*.

The marriage service was read 'with moving simplicity' by the man who had been spiritual adviser to Queen Victoria, now Archbishop of Canterbury, Dr Randall Thomas Davidson. And the Archbishop of York, Dr Cosmo Lang, gave the young couple a special address. 'The warm and generous heart of this people takes you today unto itself,' he said. 'Will you not, in response, take that heart, with all its joys and sorrows unto your own?'[16]

His words were echoed by the tumultuous cheers of the crowds that saw the Duke and Duchess of York emerge as man and wife from the Abbey and drive – this time, together, in the state coach – to their reception at Buckingham Palace. One hundred and twenty-three guests sat down to an eight-course luncheon, with no speeches in traditional royal style, just a simple toast to the bride and groom, proposed by the King.

At 4 o'clock, Bertie and Elizabeth climbed into an open landau, drawn by four greys, to drive to Waterloo station. As they left the courtyard of Buckingham Palace, the guests threw rose petals in their path – the Queen herself showering them from the balcony above, and the Prince of Wales throwing a screwed-up paper bag when he ran out of petals.

With a cavalry escort, the couple arrived at Waterloo station to board a train with a special bridal carriage upholstered in gold brocade and decorated with heather, roses, carnations and lilies of the valley. Solemnly, one of the footmen transferred to the train two odd shoes that had been tossed into their landau for luck ...

At 5.10 pm, the train drew into the country station of Bookham in Surrey, where the Duke and Duchess were to spend the first part of their honeymoon in an elegant Edwardian country house, Polesden Lacey. From there, they visited Glamis Castle, and finally Frogmore, before they took up residence in their official home at White Lodge, Richmond, the house that Queen Mary had lived in for many years as a child.

Bertie wrote to his mother: 'I do hope you will not miss me very much, though I believe you will as I have stayed with you so much longer really than the brothers.'[17] His parents felt Bertie's removal from home very keenly, but at the same time rejoiced in their new daughter. George V wrote to Bertie: 'You are indeed a lucky man to have such a charming and delightful wife as Elizabeth and I am sure you will both be very happy together and I trust you both will have many, many years of happiness before you, and that you will be as happy as Mama and I are after you have been married for 30 years, I can't wish you more ... I am quite certain that Elizabeth will be a splendid partner in your work and share with you and help you in all you have to do.'[18]

The King – like the rest of the country – had no idea when he wrote those words to his second son that a quirk of fate would make Bertie and his young Scottish commoner bride the King and Queen of England within the next ten years. But he would probably have forecast that his daughter-in-law would accept the enormous task she inherited with great composure and through her unfailing support make it possible for her husband to be King.

In his abdication speech, on 11 December 1936, Edward VIII said regretfully of his brother Bertie, the new King, 'He has one matchless blessing, enjoyed by so many of you and not bestowed on me – a happy home with his wife and children.' This was a blessing that George VI never forgot or underrated; all his life, he adored his wife, and found great comfort in her devotion to him. Theirs was a real love match.

CHAPTER FIVE

ELIZABETH AND PHILIP

The long hot summer of 1947 followed an unusually bitter winter, made worse for Britain by food rationing and fuel shortages. Two years after the war was won, clothes and petrol were still rationed, restaurants offered a choice of bread or soup, whale steak was a delicacy and utility furniture filled the shops.

But the skies no longer rained death, and the scarred cities basked in the sun like convalescents, their jagged bomb sites softened by brave clumps of mauve and golden flowers.

The announcement from Buckingham Palace in July that the twenty-one-year-old Princess Elizabeth was to marry a handsome Naval lieutenant, Philip Mountbatten, seemed a fitting climax to that lovely summer. The couple were young, good-looking and obviously in love, and the Royal Family had never been more popular.

King George VI and Queen Elizabeth had not moved from Buckingham Palace during the whole war, sharing the dangers of the Blitz and the buzz bombs with their people. When the Palace was bombed, destroying the ugly little chapel in which Princess Eliabeth had been christened, the Queen was heard to say, almost with relief, 'Now I can look the East End in the face.'

The emotional link between the people and the Throne was almost tangible. Three months before the announcement of her engagement, Princess Elizabeth had broadcast a twenty-first birthday message which was a solemn act of self-dedication: 'I declare before you all that my whole life, whether it be long or short, shall be devoted to your service and the service of our great Imperial Commonwealth to which we all belong. But I shall not have strength to carry out this resolution unless you join in it with me, as I now invite you to do; I know that your support will be unfailingly given. God bless all of you who are willing to share it.' It was a speech worthy of a great-great-granddaughter of Queen Victoria and it reflected the strong sense of public service which the young princess had inherited from her father.

The Prince of Greece, who was to share this life of dedication, was also a descendant of Queen Victoria. The fiancés were third cousins through Philip's mother – Princess Alice of Battenberg, a great-granddaughter of Queen Victoria – and second cousin once removed through Philip's father, Prince Andrew of Greece, a son of King George I of the Helenes, who was a Dane and a brother of Queen Alexandra.

Despite this relationship, and the fact that Philip had been brought up and educated largely in England, the cousins did not meet until the last summer of peace. Philip was an eighteen-year-old cadet at the Royal Naval College at Dartmouth. The King, with the Queen and the two princesses, was paying a visit to his old College. When they arrived in the royal yacht, they found Dartmouth afflicted with a combined epidemic of mumps and chicken pox. As a precaution, the two princesses were left to play in the College grounds, entertained by a party of cadets, including Philip. The Prince did his best, but he found it difficult to get a word out of his thirteen-year-old cousin who was painfully shy, and it was not a very successful first meeting.

The future Queen of England and the exiled Prince of Greece had led vastly different lives.

Elizabeth Alexandra Mary, the first child of the Duke and Duchess of York, was born in the early hours of 21 April 1926 at the Mayfair home of her maternal grandparents, the Bowes-Lyons. Her other grandmother, Queen Mary, recorded the event in her diary: 'We were awakened at 4 a.m. by Reggie Seymour, who informed us that darling Elizabeth had got a daughter . . . Such a relief and joy . . . saw the baby who is a darling with a lovely complexion and pretty fair hair.'[1] Doubtless, Queen Mary described her new granddaughter to her guest at luncheon that day, who happened to be Princess Andrew of Greece, the baby's future mother-in-law.

Lilibet, as she was to call herself, was a pretty, serene little girl and Queen Mary's favourite grandchild. The stately old lady was to be seen making sand pies in the garden with her, and she loved taking the two princesses round the sights of London.

King George V, who had been so stern with his own children, was devoted to his small grandchild. From his study window in Buckingham Palace, he could look through field glasses at the Duke of York's home in Piccadilly, and would wave to Lilibet every morning.

The King's death in 1935 may have been the first intimation to the nine-year-old girl that hers was no ordinary family. She was taken privately to Westminster Hall where the King lay in state and was much affected by the sombre ceremonial of the scene. 'Ought we to play?' she asked her governess on the day of the funeral, awed by the hushed air of mourning in the streets.

A year later, her parents' rather reluctant accession to the Throne, after the abdication of Edward VIII, changed the princess's life dramatically. But her father, mindful of his own chilly upbringing, was determined that his daughters should have a sunny, carefree childhood. They were a happy, close-knit family, though the girls were never spoiled and were taught the responsibilities of being royal at an early age.

Elizabeth in particular had a dignity at odds with her years. In May 1939 her parents sailed from Portsmouth for a seven-month tour of Canada and the United States. Queen Mary had taken the two princesses to see them off. A little shakily, Margaret turned to her sister, 'I have my handkerchief,' she said, dangerously close to tears. 'To wave, not to cry,'[2] Elizabeth replied, and Queen Mary was delighted with this early appreciation of royal behaviour.

The two sisters spent the war years between Scotland and Windsor Castle. Their parents travelled from London to be with them as often as they could, but it was a lonely, circumscribed life, with few excursions outside the massive castle walls.

There were pantomimes, film shows and informal dances and once a real adventure – an incognito trip on the London Underground. In 1945 Princess Elizabeth, eager to do some active war work, was granted an honorary commission as 'Second Subaltern Elizabeth Windsor, A.T.S.' The new subaltern, based at No 1 Mechanical Transport Training Centre at Camberley, spent her days learning to drive and cleaning the plugs of a Bedford lorry; at night, a Cinderella in reverse, she went home to her castle.

Finally, the war was over, and on that May night in 1945 when jubilant crowds milled round the Palace, the Princesses, escorted by two Guards officers, were allowed to join them. It was a never-to-be-forgotten experience of life outside the goldfish bowl, and Princess Margaret gleefully recorded knocking off a few hats and joining in the clamour for the King and Queen.

'Poor darlings, they have never had any fun yet,' the King wrote in his diary that night.[3] But the war had been enlivened for the young Elizabeth by the visits to Windsor and Balmoral of her cousin Philip, on leave from the Royal Navy. The tall, blond young man must have brought a touch of glamour, a breath of fresh air into the Princesses' small circle. And perhaps the united Royal Family gave Philip a taste of something he had not known since babyhood – a happy and settled home life.

Philip of Greece was born in an old-world villa surrounded by roses on the lush island of Corfu. He was delivered on the dining-room table, because doctors feared for the life of his thirty-six-year-old mother and thought it would give her a better chance. He was a plump, almost white-haired baby when a coup in Greece put his father's life at risk. George V sent a cruiser to pick up Prince Andrew and his wife from Phaleron Bay. The next day the children embarked from Corfu. There was no cot on board, so the future husband of the Queen of England travelled unceremoniously to exile in a converted orange box.

His parents settled briefly in Paris and Philip went to an infants school in St Cloud, while his mother ran a little shop selling Greek arts and crafts for the benefit of Greek refugees. By royal standards money was tight, but his father still had a valet, and there was a resident nurse and a lady-in-waiting for his mother.

Gradually his parents' marriage broke up. Prince Andrew went to live in the South of France and Princess Alice returned to Greece where she founded her own religious order. Philip was sent to school in England and spent his holidays with his uncle George, the 2nd Marquess of Milford Haven, and his cousin David at their home near Maidenhead.

There followed a brief spell at school in Germany. The school, run by that exceptional educationalist, Kurt Hahn, was housed in Schloss Salem, the home of the Margrave of Baden, who was married to one of Philip's sisters. Philip did not like Germany and the experiment ended with Hitler's rise to power and Kurt Hahn's imprisonment as a Jew. He was, however, fated to play a role in the Prince's life. Freed at the instigation of Ramsay MacDonald, Hahn founded a new school at Gordonstoun in Scotland, within easy reach of the sea and mountains, providing the outdoor life he advocated. Philip was one of his first pupils.

When the Prince went to Dartmouth, his former headmaster wrote these prophetic words: 'Prince Philip is a born leader, but he will need the exacting demands of a great service to do justice to himself. His best is outstanding – his second best is not good enough.'

This was the background to the young man who, by 1944, had won the affections of the greatest heiress in the world – the daughter of a King Emperor who would one day inherit the most stable throne in Europe.

The nineteen-year-old Princess was a pretty, rather diffident girl with her mother's brilliant blue eyes and her lovely complexion. But temperamentally she was more like her father, with his combination of dignity and humour, his love of sport, his common sense and his eagle eye for detail.

The slim, post-war newspapers now carried pictures of the Princess on informal visits to the theatre, on her way to private dances and dinner parties with groups of young friends. But only one photograph had pride of place on her dressing-table – that of a young man in Naval uniform, sporting a luxuriant beard and simply autographed – 'To Elizabeth, Philip.'

George VI could hardly believe that his beloved elder daughter had fallen in love with the first eligible young man she had ever met. King George of Greece had intervened on behalf of his young nephew, but the King felt that his daughter was too young to make such a momentous decision. He wrote to Queen Mary: 'We both think she is too young for that now, as she has never met any young men of her own age.' But he added: 'I like Philip. He is intelligent, has a good sense of humour & thinks about things in the right way ... We are going to tell George that P. had better not think any more about it for the present.'[4]

The young couple were not put off by the King's rebuff and went on seeing one another – at Coppins, the home of the widowed

Marina of Kent, Philip's cousin, and at the Sunningdale house of a younger cousin, Alexandra, who had married the former King Peter of Yugoslavia.

Meanwhile, Philip was pressing to become a British subject. The King, who was a stickler for correctness, had insisted that the King of Greece should give his approval. This was obtained in 1944, but because of political unrest in Greece the matter was shelved. The King was prepared to allow Philip to style himself 'His Royal Highness, Prince Philip,' and was impressed when the young man said he would prefer to be simply Lieutenant Philip Mountbatten, RN.

By 1946, Philip had proposed privately and been accepted. Alas, there is as yet no diary like Victoria's to record the scene for us, but the Queen in later years admitted that it happened in Scotland, 'beside some well-loved loch, the white clouds sailing overhead and the curlew crying.' But the King refused to give his consent until the Royal Family's tour of South Africa was over – a separation of four months for the young couple.

For the Princess, whatever her feelings, the tour was to prove a fairytale experience of sunshine and cheers. After the years of austerity, the official dinners seemed so enormous that the Queen had to ask for smaller menus, and diamonds were presented almost as casually as flowers. The Princess was given a boxful when she opened a dock in East London. There were diamonds in Kimberley for both sisters and when Elizabeth came of age in Cape Town, South Africa's gift was a casket of twenty-one beautiful stones.

Meanwhile in England Lord Louis Mountbatten and his wife Edwina, Philip's glamorous uncle and aunt, were doing their best to smooth the way for their nephew's wedding to the heir to the throne. The King was still concerned about the nation's reaction to the match. All Philip's sisters were married to former German Army officers. One of them, Prince Christopher of Hesse, had taken part in raids on Britain. In 1947 the scars left by those raids were still visible.

While the Royal Family were sailing to South Africa, the Mountbattens invited the chairman of Beaverbrook newspapers and the editors of the *Daily Express* and the *Sunday Express* to drinks at their London home. It was a subtle and surprising move. For years

Lord Beaverbrook had conducted a campaign against Mountbatten in his newspapers.

While Philip sat in the background of the pretty sitting-room, his uncle and aunt asked the newspapermen for their reaction to the young man's taking British nationality. Their answer was unanimous – in view of his war record, his ties with the Royal Family and his English upbringing, they could see no grounds for public disapproval. It was a victory for the Mountbattens' diplomacy – a possible source of opposition had been silenced by consultation.

Things then moved quickly. In March, Philip renounced his membership of the Greek and Danish royal families and became plain Lieutenant Mountbatten, to a background of engagement rumours. In May, the Royal Family, with a radiant Princess Elizabeth, were back in England, and on 10 July a Palace statement announced the engagement between the £11-a-week naval lieutenant and the King's daughter.

If Philip had any illusions about what his future held, they must have been dispelled by the solemn tone of the leading article in The Times: 'A new career in the service of King and Commonwealth now opens out before this tried and distinguished young officer ... the position of consort to the next Sovereign of the British Empire ... a position of great difficulty, much delicacy, heavy responsibility ... the future Queen will have to look to him as her principal support and helper in every aspect of her life's work.' They were sobering words for a young man of twenty-five to read on the morning of his engagement to a pretty girl of twenty-one. On a happier note, Queen Mary recorded in her diary: 'Heard with great pleasure of darling Lilibet's engagement to Philip Mountbatten. They both came to see me after luncheon looking radiant.'5 The old Queen had a soft spot for Philip, and enjoyed his naughty naval stories.

The wedding, fixed for 20 November in Westminster Abbey, was to be as like as possible to that of the bride's parents, though in keeping with the mood of austerity. There were some sour notes. The London District TUC passed a resolution urging the Government 'to prevent any dislocation of labour and materials by regarding this wedding purely as the domestic concern of the persons involved'. With more vision and sense of history, Winston Churchill gauged the mood of the public. 'Millions will welcome this joyous event as a flash of colour on the hard road we have to travel.' That it was to be, as well as a demonstration to the world at large of the stability of Britain's ancient institutions. As one foreign guest was to say after the wedding: 'A nation which can throw such a party as that will never go under.'

But in the meantime there were more mundane and penny-pinching considerations. Parliament voted the Princess an increased annuity of £50,000 and Philip a special annuity of £10,000 a year. This was a third of the sum which had so insulted Victoria's consort 100 years earlier, when money was worth far more than in post-war Britain. But the King voluntarily gave up £100,000 from the Civil List savings made during the war to pay the initial expenses of the Princess's establishment, and paid most of the wedding expenses from the Privy Purse.

It was thanks to the Labour War Minister, Emmanuel Shinwell, that the Princess had a fitting escort: for the first time since the war the Household Cavalry were to wear full dress uniform for the wedding.

Even the Princess's engagement ring had a make-do-and-mend touch about it. It was re-designed from a ring which belonged to Philip's mother – a square diamond, set in platinum flanked with two baguette diamonds.

But there was no austerity about the wedding gifts which poured in from all over the world – a gold-encrusted coffee service from the Emir of Transjordan; a full-length mink coat from Canada; a fabulous necklace of ninety-six rubies in a gold setting from Burma – each ruby a charm against the ninety-six diseases of Burmese lore. A filly arrived from the Aga Khan and a Siamese kitten from a district nurse; a grand piano from the RAF and a wastepaper basket from 'Bobo' Macdonald, the Princess's dresser and friend. On a practical note, the WVS sent a refrigerator and there were enough electric toasters, kettles and vacuum cleaners to equip several homes. Princess Margaret gave her sister a fully-fitted picnic basket; someone sent a pastel portrait of the royal corgis and Mahatma Gandhi sent a piece of crochet lace, worked by himself.

From the Royal Family there was a collection of fabulous jewellery – a ruby and diamond necklace and two pearl necklaces from the King and Queen; a diamond tiara, a diamond stomacher eight inches deep, bracelets and a brooch from Queen Mary (they had been her own wedding presents). And there were cases of silver, glass and gold plate. How it must have sparkled in the drabness of post-war London as people queued for days to see the gifts displayed in St James's Palace! And for the first time in history, a King's daughter received a gift of food parcels – 32,000 of them from America. They were distributed to needy widows with a personal letter from the Princess.

Cloak-and-dagger secrecy surrounded the design of the wedding dress by Norman Hartnell, who not only curtained his work-room windows but also white-washed the glass. There was a small flurry in those days of post-war patriotism and import permits when it was rumoured that Hartnell was using French silk for the dress. A statement hastily issued traced the silk to Chinese silkworms, whose efforts had been woven in Scotland and Kent.

In November the King wrote to Queen Mary: 'I am giving the Garter to Lilibet next Tuesday, November 11th, so that she will be senior to Philip, to whom I am giving it on November 19th. I have arranged that he shall be created a Royal Highness and that the titles of his peerage will be Baron Greenwich, Earl of Merioneth & Duke of Edinburgh. It is a great deal to give a man all at once, but I know Philip understands his new responsibilities on his marriage to Lilibet.'[6]

A few days before the wedding, the royal guests began to arrive for the largest gathering of royalty of the century. The state apartments of the Palace were opened after eight years for a dinner party for kings and queens. And the following evening, over 1,000 guests were invited to a party at the Palace. How Queen Mary loved it all! She wrote: 'Saw many old friends, I stood from 9.30 till 12.15 am!! not bad for 80.'[7] It was rather as though the most exclusive club in the world were holding a reunion.

The evening before the wedding, as Prince Philip prepared to set off for his stag party at the Dorchester, Londoners, with blankets, vacuum flasks and sleeping bags, began to camp out in the chilly November evening to make sure of a vantage-point along the procession's route.

The wedding day dawned dull and misty over a city swarming with people. Thousands had saved their petrol to drive up for the day and some 1,600 reporters and photographers from all over the world had arrived to cover the wedding which *The Times* called 'a family event transacted in the bosom of history.'

At Buckingham Palace there were small last-minute dramas. The Princess's diamond tiara broke and had to be rushed to a jeweller for a quick repair. The bridal bouquet could not be found and the pearl necklace she was to wear almost failed to arrive from St James's Palace. Small wonder the ladies from Hartnell who helped to dress the bride found her pale and very solemn.

But by 10.45 the first procession was ready to leave Buckingham Palace for the Abbey – members of the Royal Family and visiting royalty. Half an hour later, the groom and his best man and cousin, Lord Milford Haven, arrived at the Abbey, and the two young men slipped discreetly through Poet's Corner into the church.

The third procession left from Marlborough House, with Queen Mary flying her own standard. At the west door of the Abbey she was joined by the Queen who had travelled from the palace with Princess Margaret, the chief bridesmaid, in a glass coach, escorted by a Captain's Escort of the Household Cavalry.

Promptly at 11.16 the bride's procession wound out of the Palace courtyard, the Princess and her father in the Irish State Coach, followed by members of the Household and a Sovereign's Escort of Household Cavalry resplendent in full uniform. How the crowds cheered at the colour and splendour of it all in the grey November day!

In the Abbey, the guests were now assembled. Only a few had seats in the sacrarium and a full view of the ceremony. They included members of the Cabinet and Opposition and representatives of Commonwealth and Empire. There was a moving moment when Winston Churchill entered the Abbey alone and the whole congregation rose to him spontaneously.

The mothers of the bride and groom walked slowly up the aisle together, Philip's mother having discarded the severe garb of her order for just one day. Queen Mary, a stately figure in blue, followed, accompanied by the King of Norway. Next came the procession of visiting clergy – the two Archbishops of Canterbury and York, with their white and gold mitres, their crosses carried before them.

At the west door of the Abbey, the Collegium of the church waited for their sovereign and the bride: the Dean and Chapter, the lay vicars, the choristers and the King's scholars. High up in the ancient walls a fanfare of silver trumpets sounded and the entire college bowed as the King entered, his daughter on his arm.

According to the custom of royal brides, the Princess was not veiled. *The Times* was to describe her as looking happy and 'singularly childlike' in her Botticelli-inspired dress, a description which is borne out by the photographs of the day, showing her in the dress of pearl-coloured satin, with its long, tight sleeves, heart-shaped neckline and full skirt. Ten thousand costume pearls and crystals had gone into the embroidery of garlands of white York roses with ears of corn, a design repeated in the 15ft bridal train.

The two little pages, Prince William of Gloucester and Prince Michael of Kent, wore white shirts and tartan kilts, and the eight bridesmaids, who were related to either bride or groom, included Princess Margaret and Princess Alexandra of Kent.

As the procession walked up the aisle, the choir sang the Princess's own choice of music – first the well-loved 'Praise my soul, the King of Heaven'. When the last note died away, Princess Margaret stepped forward to take her sister's bouquet of white orchids and carnations.

The Dean of Westminster, bowing to the King, began the service. As the Archbishop of Canterbury spoke the solemn words, 'who giveth this woman?', the King reached out for the Princess's right hand and symbolically handed her over. The low, clear voices of the bride and groom were relayed to the silent crowds outside the Abbey, to the thousands with portable radios along the route, and to the millions listening at home.

The Archbishop of York delivered the address and the service ended with the blessing by the Archbishop of Canterbury and one verse of the National Anthem. While the register was being signed in the Chapel of Edward the Confessor, the banners of the Abbey were brought out into the sanctuary, facing the door of the shrine.

26 Lady Elizabeth Bowes-Lyon with her eldest brother, Lord Glamis (left) and her father, the Earl of Strathmore, taken just before her marriage

27 The wedding in Westminster Abbey, 26 April 1923

28 The marriage register

29 The newlywed couple, by Bassano

30 The first engagement picture of Princess Elizabeth and Prince Philip

31 (*above left*) Princess Elizabeth and Prince Philip in the days of their courtship

32 (*above right*) Leaving Westminster Abbey after the marriage ceremony, 20 November 1947

33 The radiant princess with her bridegroom in the carriage on their way to the reception

34 (*below*) Princess Elizabeth waves to the crowds from the balcony of Buckingham Palace

20 November 1947

1	Prince George of Denmark	15	Duchess of Aosta	30 Princess Elizabeth
2	Princess George of Greece	16	Hereditary Prince of Luxemburg	31 Duke of Edinburgh
3	King Peter of Yugo Slavia	17	Princess Eugenie of Greece	32 Princess Alexandra of Kent
4	Queen Alexandra of Yugo Slavia	18	Lady Milford Haven	33 The King
5	Lord Mountbatten of Burma	19	Princess Andrew of Greece	34 The Queen
6	Count of Barcelona	20	Lady Mountbatten of Burma	35 Duke of Gloucester
7	Prince Bernhard of the Netherlands	21	Duchess of Kent	36 Duchess of Gloucester
8	King of Norway	22	Princess Juliana of the Netherlands	37 Princess Rene of Bourbon Parma
9	Prince Charles of Belgium	23	Queen of Greece	38 Princess Marie Louise
10	Prince George of Greece	24	Queen Mary	39 Crown Prince of Sweden
11	Prince Rene of Bourbon Parma	25	Queen Victoria Eugenie	40 Prince William of Gloucester
12	King of Denmark	26	Queen of Denmark	41 Prince Michael of Kent
13	King of Roumania	27	Crown Princess of Sweden	42 Prince Richard of Gloucester
14	Prince Michael of Bourbon Parma	28	Princess Margaret	43 Princess Helena Victoria
		29	Lord Milford Haven	

35 Inside Buckingham Palace

36 A twenty-ninth birthday picture of Princess Margaret, taken by her fiancé

37 Princess Margaret (centre) with the Queen at Badminton in April 1953; Peter Townsend stands on the left

38 (*below*) Princess Margaret with her fiancé, Anthony Armstrong-Jones, reading the telegrams of congratulations at Royal Lodge, Windsor

39 The joining of hands by the Archbishop of Canterbury, Westminster Abbey, 14 May 1960

40 Princess Margaret on the balcony which leads from the Green Room at
Buckingham Palace

41 Anne and Mark in the grounds of Buckingham Palace following the announcement of their engagement

42 (*top*) The engagement day: (left to right) Prince Philip, Captain Mark Phillips, Princess Anne, Mrs Phillips, the Queen and Mr Peter Phillips

43 (*above*) Captain Phillips adjusting Princess Anne's stock

44 In the Long Gallery at Windsor Castle, a week before the marriage

45 Inside Buckingham Palace after the wedding ceremony

46 (*above*) The traditional balcony scene at Buckingham Palace

47 Princess Anne and Captain Phillips in Quito, Ecuador, where they spent part of their honeymoon

The silver trumpets pealed again from the chantry of Henry V, and the bride and groom emerged smiling and hand-in-hand. In a touching token of respect, they curtseyed and bowed deeply before Queen Mary.

As they walked out of the Abbey, to the sound of Mendelssohn's 'Wedding March', it was 12.30 precisely – a touch of that almost military precision which marks a British royal wedding. The Princess had meant to leave her bouquet on the grave of the Unknown Soldier in the same moving gesture as her mother, but she forgot and the flowers were brought back to the Abbey the next day.

At the Palace, there were 10,000 telegrams of congratulations and 1,000 carnations and boxes of mimosa which had arrived as a gift from the South of France. One hundred and fifty people sat down to the wedding breakfast in the gold and white supper room of the Palace, decorated with white heather and pink carnations. There were touches of family history – the flowers on the centre table included sprigs of myrtle, grown from the myrtle in Queen Victoria's bouquet, and as the pipers from Balmoral played, the Princess and her husband cut the wedding cake with his grandfather's sword.

At 3.50 there were more cheers from the waiting crowds, as the Princess and her husband left in an open landau for Waterloo station. In her coat and dress of love-in-the-mist blue, Elizabeth sat in a cosy nest of hot-water bottles, her pet corgi, Crackers, at her feet. They were bound for Broadlands, the Mountbatten home in the New Forest, for the first part of the honeymoon.

According to the *Daily Mail*, the newly-weds 'did not dress for dinner. The menu was vegetable soup, roast chicken, followed by coffee and brandy.' The Romsey police had to be augmented to keep a constant look-out for foreign photographers, and before Elizabeth and Philip moved to the greater seclusion of Birkhall on the Balmoral estate, for the second part of their honeymoon, they issued this statement in which one may read a touch of gentle irony: 'Before we leave for Scotland tonight we want to say the reception given us on our wedding day and the loving interest shown by our fellow countrymen and well-wishers in all parts of the world have left an impression which will never grow faint. We can find no words to express what we feel, but we can at least offer our grateful thanks to the millions who have given us this unforgettable send-off in our married life.'

The King felt the separation from his daughter keenly. He wrote to her during her honeymoon: 'I was so proud of you & thrilled at having you so close to me on our long walk in Westminster Abbey, but when I handed your hand to the Archbishop I felt that I had lost something very precious. You were so calm & composed during the Service & said your words with such conviction, that I knew everything was all right.'[8]

And then comes a revealing glimpse into the close relationship of the Royal Family: 'I am so glad you wrote & told Mummy that you think the long wait before your engagement ... was for the best. I was rather afraid that you had thought I was being hardhearted about it ... Our family, us four, the "Royal Family" must remain together with additions of course at suitable moments!! I have watched you grow up all these years with pride under the skilful direction of Mummy, who as you know is the most marvellous person in the World, in my eyes, & I can, I know always count on you, & now Philip to help us in our work. Your leaving us has left a great blank in our lives but do remember that your old home is still yours & do come back to it as much & as often as possible. I can see that you are sublimely happy with Philip which is right but don't forget us is the wish of

Your ever loving & devoted Papa.'[9]

The next four years of married life were happy, carefree and fulfilling for the Princess. They saw the birth of Prince Charles and Princess Anne, and happy days spent at the Mountbattens' villa in Malta where the Duke of Edinburgh was in command of the frigate *Magpie*. Here the Princess was free to swim, picnic on the beach, shop and have her hair done like other naval wives.

So the King's sudden death at Sandringham in 1952 was not just a sad personal loss to a devoted daughter. It meant that the twenty-five-year-old Princess was now the first Queen Regnant since Victoria, and, in the words of *Life* magazine, well on the way to becoming the 'most overworked young woman this side of the Iron Curtain'.

CHAPTER SIX

PRINCESS MARGARET

'It is with great pleasure that Queen Elizabeth the Queen Mother announces the betrothal of her beloved daughter the Princess Margaret to Mr Antony Armstrong-Jones, son of Mr Ronald Armstrong-Jones, Q.C., and the Countess of Rosse, to which union the Queen has gladly given her consent.'

This court circular issued from Clarence House in January 1960 took the world generally by surprise, and for the first time in ten years silenced the gossip and speculation that had surrounded Princess Margaret's romances.

Margaret Rose was born in Scotland – the first member of the Royal Family to be born there for more than 300 years – in the middle of a raging storm. The birth took place at Glamis Castle, at the wish of her mother, the Duchess of York, who chose her old family home first for its sentimental ties but also to please her countrymen. The Scots were delighted. On the night of 21 August, 1930, when Princess Margaret Rose was born, the celebrations throughout the country were fantastic. At Glamis itself – 'The Glamis pipe band, in full dress, piped the villagers to the top of Hunter's Hill, two miles from the Castle, for the lighting of the beacon which had been built to celebrate the event. At the summit two large barrels of beer had been taken up to enable the foresters, ploughmen and others to drink the health of the infant Princess. Three village girls from Glamis lit the beacon with torches . . . The pile burned fiercely and could be seen by watchers in six counties. Hundreds of Scottish folk joined hands, danced round the beacon and burst into cheers. The bagpipes played "Highland Lassie" and a piece specially composed for the occasion, "The Duke of York's Welcome".' (*The Times*).

Inside the castle the family celebrated too: Margaret's grandparents, Lord and Lady Strathmore, her aunt, Lady Rose Leveson-Gower, her father, the Duke of York.

None was more pleased at the royal birth than the Home Secretary. Required by tradition to be present, Mr Clynes had anticipated the happy event by some days in his eagerness, and had been spending a restless time with relations of the Bowes-Lyons. He describes the scene of the birth: 'I went to the cot and peeping in I saw a fine, chubby-faced little girl lying wide awake ... The Duke of York was obviously delighted and Lord and Lady Strathmore stood with smiling faces gazing down at the baby. On behalf of the nation and the Empire as a whole I congratulated the Duke and also the Duchess's parents.'[1] Clynes at once telegraphed the world with the news, adding 'The infant Princess is doing fine.' A few days later, Sir Henry Simpson, the surgeon who assisted at the birth, amplified: 'I am able today,' he said, 'to give some particulars of the Royal baby which will be of interest to mothers everywhere. Her eyes like those of her Royal parents, of the King and Queen, and also of her grandparents, the Earl and Countess of Strathmore are a vivid blue tending to lightness. Her hair is of a tint between light and medium brown. The shape of her lips already shows a marked resemblance to that of her mother's. She is a remarkably contented baby but when she does cry she gives ample proof of her possession of lusty lungs.'[2]

The celebrations and the summer storm were not unprophetic of Margaret's life in later years. However, her childhood began in a peaceful, protected fashion. The Duke of York and his family lived in the Royal Lodge at Windsor, in a charming house enclosed by lavender hedges. Both the Duke and Duchess were keen gardeners and the little princesses were allowed small plots to tend.

Geoffrey Wakeford describes their first years as 'Tea at Windsor Castle, birthdays at Balmoral with angel cake sent up specially from Glamis, tremulous approaches to King George's shy little Cairn terrier, Bob, readings out of nursery books in which Margaret could readily identify a Welsh dragon with the Loch Ness Monster, visits to Grandma at St. Paul's among the knobbly oaks and the ilex trees, romps with Ianto, the Welsh terrier who guarded the little thatched house, readings from *Peter Pan* by the great James Barrie himself, who once described Princess Margaret as "the most gracious lady in the land", a glorious garden party in the grounds of Glamis Castle to celebrate the golden wedding of Lord and Lady Strathmore ... [The Duchess of York] dressed her children in little cherry-red coats, or sent them to parties in frocks of pink and blue sprigged muslin, with frilled bonnets to match, or in pastel shaded chiffon with white fur coats.'³

Margaret's first official appearance was when she was five years old, as a bridesmaid to an old friend of her mother's. Her sister 'Lilibet' was also bridesmaid, and apparently the two little girls stole the show. Already, they were showing signs of very different characters. Elizabeth was more serious; intensely loyal and aware of her responsibilities to the extent of keeping a watchful eye on her younger sister. Margaret was fun-loving, fond of playing the fool, with an enchanting smile just like her mother's.

The Duchess of York was careful to keep her children out of the limelight as much as possible, but the newspapers followed their activities with a keen interest, accentuated by their uncle's dramatic abdication in 1936. Now Elizabeth, aged nine, was first in line of succession to the throne, and Margaret second. From that moment, their lives were to become virtually public property.

The war meant separations for the closely-knit Royal Family. The girls spent their time between Windsor and Scotland; the King and Queen were with them as often as possible but their duties took them to London or elsewhere. It was a lonely time for two spirited teenagers, but during the war they both made momentous meetings that were later to affect their lives. In 1939 Princess Elizabeth, aged thirteen, met the man she was to marry, and in 1944 Princess Margaret, also at thirteen, met the man she was to fall in love with – Group Captain Peter Townsend, Equerry to the King.

At the end of the war the Royal Family resumed normal life at Buckingham Palace, with frequent stays at Windsor Castle. The King and Queen tried to make up to their children for the fun they had lost as teenagers in the war years, and encouraged the girls to make friends outside the Palace circle and to entertain at home.

Princess Elizabeth's romance with Philip of Greece flourished; they were engaged and married in 1947, with Princess Margaret as their chief bridesmaid. By now, Princess Margaret was seventeen.

77

Her sparkling wit, ability to play hit tunes on the piano by ear, her powers of mimicry (inherited from her mother's side of the family) and her lively charm had made her many friends. She had her own suite at the Palace where she gave small informal parties and dinners.

One of her closest companions was a bubbling American, Sharman Douglas, daughter of the American ambassador in London. Together, the Princess and Sharman introduced a breath of modern air into Buckingham Palace's traditional corridors, in the form of top singers and cabaret artistes such as Danny Kaye.

Princess Margaret's father, the King, was very close to her always. In 1948 he was a sick man, and over the following four years his condition slowly deteriorated. But Margaret could make him laugh, or coax him from a gloomy mood by singing gay songs at the piano. The last big family party before his death was Margaret's twenty-first birthday. Despite his condition, the King was determined that his youngest daughter should enjoy her coming of age, and the Queen gave a big dance at Windsor. Margaret, looking dazzling in a white Dior dress with a full skirt embroidered with crystals, danced the night away with her friends.

The newspapers were avidly interested in the Princess's private life: they had christened her friends 'the Margaret Set', and constantly linked her name with new suitors – none of whom appeared to last longer than a fortnight. However, the gossip columnists overlooked one young man who was often at her side – the King's good-looking Equerry, Peter Townsend.

Margaret and Peter had first met in 1944, outside her father's study, when he was twenty-nine and she was thirteen. Peter was a hero of the Battle of Britain. Twice decorated by his king, he had been the first to shoot down a German bomber over Britain and was credited with destroying eleven other enemy planes. His appointment as Equerry had stemmed from the King's admiration for the young men who were helping to win the war.

A bond of real friendship had grown up between the King and his Equerry. Peter and his wife were given a grace and favour house in Windsor Great Park, and when their second son was born, the King agreed to be godfather. However, Peter's wife, Rosemary, found that his duties at the Palace made her a 'Palace Widow' for weeks on end. Finally, she left him, in 1951, taking their two sons. The Townsend divorce a year later made only a small paragraph in the newspapers.

When the King died, in February 1952, Margaret turned to Peter Townsend to comfort her in her grief. It was the beginning of a love affair that burst like a bombshell at the Queen's coronation, six months later, when journalists and television viewers alike could not mistake the bond of affection between the Princess and the Group Captain.

Their romance had painful echoes of Edward VIII's affair with Mrs Simpson, sixteen years previously. The Queen Mother was aware of her daughter's feelings and sympathised greatly with the lovers. So did the Queen. Yet Townsend was a divorcee, and the Queen as head of the Church could not recognise his second marriage even if it was to her younger sister. With tact and delicacy, the Queen Mother tried to break up the relationship, finally deciding that the best course was to separate the lovers.

Townsend should have accompanied the Queen Mother and Princess Margaret on an official tour of Central Africa, but another equerry took his place. Townsend was sent to Brussels, and on the African tour the sad Princess suffered from a constant stream of minor ailments – colds, flu, bugs – which kept her in bed, leaving the Queen Mother to carry out their engagements for the most part alone.

The period of trial separation for the lovers lasted twenty-eight months. In August 1955 Princess Margaret celebrated her twenty-fifth birthday, and was constitutionally free to marry whom she pleased. But it had been made quite clear to her that to choose Group Captain Townsend meant relinquishing all her rights, as her uncle had done before her.

The world watched and waited for the Princess to choose between love and duty. Early in October Margaret travelled from Balmoral to London, while Townsend made his way from Belgium to meet her. For the next three weeks the drama was played out while the young couple, besieged by reporters and photographers, saw each other briefly at Clarence House and at dinner parties specially given by the Princess's closest friends.

There was to be no happy ending. At the end of October Margaret went to see the Archbishop of Canterbury, Dr Geoffrey Fisher, who had his Bible and reference books ready to help. Sadly, she said to him: 'Archbishop, you may put your books away, I have made up my mind.' With the help of the Group Captain, at the country home of Lord Rupert Nevill, she drafted her own communiqué to the world, on 3 October. Even eighteen years later, it is a document moving in its simplicity:

'I would like it to be known that I have decided not to marry Group Captain Peter Townsend. I have been aware that, subject to my renouncing my rights of succession, it might have been possible for me to contract a civil marriage. But mindful of the Church's teaching that Christian marriage is indissoluble and conscious of my duty to the Commonwealth, I have resolved to put these considerations before any others. I have reached this decision entirely alone, and in doing so I have been strengthened by the support and devotion of Group Captain Townsend. I am deeply grateful for the concern of all those who have constantly prayed for my happiness.'

Peter Townsend returned to Brussels and, in 1959, married Marie-Luce Jamagne, a twenty-one-year-old Belgian girl whom the papers reported as looking remarkably like the Princess he had lost. Princess Margaret continued to play her royal role in public life; in private, she sought solace in the company of her many friends.

A year passed with no hint of a new royal romance. Then, one week after the birth of the Queen's third son, Andrew, the Princess's engagement was announced. The Queen Mother's communiqué from Clarence House took the world by surprise; the royal romance had been a brilliantly kept secret. Little was known about the prospective bridegroom except that he was famous as a photographer, for work that included several portraits of members of the Royal Family.

His name was Antony Armstrong-Jones. 'Tony' as the Press quickly discovered, lived and worked in a studio basement in Pimlico, using as his 'country residence' a dockland house in Rotherhithe. His background was similar to that of many sons of wealthy parents. Eton, then Jesus College, Cambridge, where he studied architecture for two years and coxed the winning boat race crew in 1956.

In 1957, to his mother's dismay, Tony had decided to abandon architecture in favour of his hobby, photography. He went to serve his apprenticeship under the eminent portrait photographer, Baron, before setting up his own studio in Pimlico.

His first royal assignment came as a result of his application to the Palace to take the official portraits of the Duke of Kent on his coming of age in 1955. On the Duke's subsequent recommendation, Tony photographed Prince Charles and Princess Anne a year later – charming, informal studies that showed a real break with the traditional, formal Royal Family pictures. But despite his business connections with the Palace, Tony did not meet Princess Margaret until 1958, at a private dinner party in Cheyne Walk, Chelsea.

The photographer and the princess found out immediately that they had much in common, including a love of theatre, jazz, clothes, art and almost anything new. Soon after that first meeting, they were photographed together (in a party of six) at London's latest musical, 'West Side Story'. From then onwards, though they met frequently, they were generally able to avoid the curious eye of the world.

Tony's Rotherhithe hideaway where he did the cooking – chiefly steaks or spaghetti – was their favourite rendezvous. Together, he and the Princess would wander through the streets incognito; just another young man in an open-necked shirt with his girl friend – only slightly disguised by dark glasses and a headscarf.

Two years from the time of their first meeting, Princess Margaret and her fiancé sat in the Queen Mother's sitting-room at the Royal Lodge, sipping champagne and listening to the radio announcement of their engagement. The date was 26 February 1960. Their wedding day was arranged for 14 May, later that year – only two and a half months in which to make the arrangements for receiving over 2,000 guests at the Abbey and 100 friends and relations at the Palace for a wedding breakfast. In addition to the usual fervour of wedding preparations was the added complication that this was to be the first-ever televised royal wedding.

The Princess, who wrote to a friend happily 'Never before have two people been so much in love', chose Norman Hartnell to design her wedding dress and the bridesmaids' dresses. In a poignant tribute to her father, she asked Hartnell to follow his design for her first evening dress which had been a great favourite with the late king. Accordingly, the bridesmaids' dresses were frilly, with puff sleeves, *broderie anglaise* panels, and touches of blue lace.

By contrast, the Princess's wedding dress was superbly simple, with a tight-fitting bodice and high V-neckline. It was made of white silk organza, the top layer taking thirty yards of fabric, over a stiffened tulle underskirt. Her only ornament was a magnificent diamond tiara. Her wedding ring, a plain gold band, was made from the same Welsh nugget that had produced wedding rings for her mother and her sister. It showed off beautifully her engagement ring: a chunky brilliant ruby, surrounded by diamonds, in the shape of a flower.

The bridegroom chose gold travelling clocks, in bright red leather cases, inscribed with the date, to give to the eight bridesmaids. For their part, the young couple received hundreds of presents from all over the world – including a 30lb block of chocolate in the shape of a wedding telegram, and a special recording of a tune written for the occasion by their friend, Count Basie. Eleven wedding cakes arrived at the Palace and were later distributed to hospitals and the needy; the official cake for the Reception had been ordered by the Queen Mother: it stood over 6ft high and weighed more than 10 stone.

Preparations for the big day were accompanied by the inevitable problems that surround any wedding, small or large, and the glare of publicity that focuses on all royal occasions. The Press (especially foreign papers) chose to hint at hidden scandals and a number of reporters seized upon perfectly understandable and legitimate refusals from foreign royals as 'snubs' . . .

But if the Press did not care to smile on the royal wedding, at least the sun did, and the morning of 14 May dawned fine and clear. Many of the crowd had been waiting to keep their vantage viewpoints since the night before, along with the police who were there to control them, the TV technicians who were to transmit the wedding to an estimated 300 million viewers throughout Europe and North America, and those responsible for the magnificent floral displays. The greatest of these was a four-span arch across the Mall at a point between Clarence House and the Victoria Memorial; it contained mainly fresh flowers, and many roses as a compliment to the bride, Margaret Rose. But other floral displays along the royal route also included a further 5,000 roses and hydrangeas. The Abbey was filled with fresh flower arrangements in shades of yellow and white, and was opened to the public for twenty-four hours before the wedding, during which time the bride's bouquet of orchids and other flowers lay on a purple cushion on the altar steps.

The guests began arriving at the Abbey to take their places from nine am. People from all walks of life, ranging from Mrs Peabody who had been Tony's 'char' for many years, to Sir Winston and Lady Churchill; Sir Anthony and Lady Eden; the cream of British aristocracy; and celebrities such as Noel Coward, Jean Cocteau, Joyce Grenfell, John Betjeman and John Cranko who represented the bride and groom's friends in the literary and show business worlds. Anne Scott James summed up the fashion scene, the following day:

'The big story, of course, was the hats – there must have been at least a thousand new hats that day at the Abbey. The prettiest were toques or muffins of crushed tulle, there were small helmets of flowers, there were beehive hats of light crinoline straw. There were very few large hats to spoil the view of the guests in the row behind, but neither were there any half hats ... they were properly constructed.

'The second story was the beauty of the colours, which were plain, light and luscious. The most important was yellow, the same lucid yellow that the Princess wore for her going-away dress ... Print dresses were few and those decently blurred ... I must admit that I was dazzled by the British men. If I could have chosen one to escort me I would have been torn between Lord David Cecil, almost any bishop in gaiters (*how* those bishops can dress) and Lord Dalkeith ... The Duke of Edinburgh won my admiration with a pink carnation of a size and brilliance rarely seen outside the tops of packets.'

The Duke also won the hearts of those who saw him joke with his sister-in-law as he took her to the altar, managing to coax a happy smile from her and calm her natural pre-wedding nerves. Chief bridesmaid, following immediately in their footsteps, was a plump, nine-year-old Princess Anne, for whom the Duke was to play the same role at her wedding to Mark Phillips, thirteen years later.

Waiting for the bridal procession by the side of the altar was the remainder of the Royal Family; the Queen Mother resplendent in white and gold lamé; Prince Charles wearing a kilt and sporran; and the bride's sister, the Queen, wearing the colour that perhaps suits her best, bright turquoise, but looking pale and solemn. (Again, the Press were quick to point this out next day, perhaps without knowing that Her Majesty was suffering from flu and a temperature and had got up from her sickbed to attend the wedding.)

It took little over an hour for the Princess to become Her Royal Highness Mrs Armstrong-Jones, and for the erstwhile court photographer to become a member of the Royal Family. Then, hand-in-hand, smiling confidently and very happily, the bride and groom left the Abbey to drive in the glass coach along the sunlit Mall to the Palace. The rapturous crowd cheered their procession all the way, and for long after the balcony appearances yelled their appreciation of a beautiful bride and the husband of her choice.

Thousands saw the Princess and Tony, covered in rose-petal confetti, drive in an open Daimler to Tower Pier to board the Queen's yacht *Britannia* for their honeymoon in the Caribbean. The Princess wore – appropriately enough – a sunshine yellow pure silk shantung coat, cut straight and loose with a small stand-away collar and three-quarter-length sleeves. In a wifely gesture, she brushed away the confetti on her husband's blue suit as they waved a smiling good-bye to the crowds at the docks.

There must have been many among the millions watching – there and on TV – who remembered the sad-faced Princess and her unhappy romance in 1955 and made a special wish for her future happiness.

Paperback publisher's note: This text was written in 1975.

CHAPTER SEVEN

PRINCESS ANNE

On a bleak February day in 1840, a small number of carefully selected guests endured the cold in the Chapel Royal of St James's Palace to see Queen Victoria married to her cousin, Albert. One hundred and thirty-three years later, her great-great-great-granddaughter, Princess Anne, walked down the aisle of Westminster Abbey watched by over 500 million people, at the most public royal wedding the world has ever seen.

It is a curious paradox that as the significance of royal weddings has diminished, the pomp and pageantry surrounding them has become inflated. For monarchy today is not a 'growth industry'. The thrones of Europe which Victoria and Albert so zealously helped to fill are mostly empty. The cumbersome bureaucracy of the Common Market has replaced merger by royal marriage, and princesses are no longer valued pawns on the chessboard of European diplomacy.

But a British royal wedding – that curious mixture of cosy family occasion and state pageantry – still makes excellent material for a television spectacular, in full colour with plenty of star names and a cast of thousands. It's good for business too – Princess Anne's wedding filled hotels and restaurants and sold over £6 million worth of souvenirs – and provides a shot in the arm for morale. The Princess's wedding briefly lightened the gloom of Britain's worst economic crisis in years, just as her parents' in 1947 brought a welcome flash of colour and public rejoicing after the war.

Like her mother, the Queen, Anne was clearly marrying for love; like her aunt Princess Margaret and her cousin Princess Alexandra, she was marrying a commoner. As she knelt with her handsome bridegroom, Captain Mark Phillips of the Queen's Dragoon Guards, in the ancient Abbey, the scene of so much history, she formed a living link between royal traditions that are centuries old and the fast-moving world of the seventies.

Writing about Princess Elizabeth's wedding in her book *My Memories of Six Reigns*, Princess Marie Louise, a granddaughter of Queen Victoria, expressed a wish that 'Queen Victoria could have known this great-great-great-granddaughter of hers; they would have had so much in common, and I do not think that modern life as represented to her by Lilibet would have displeased or shocked her.'[1]

One feels less sure about the old Queen's reactions to the baby who, in 1950, wearing Victoria's own christening robe, was named Anne Elizabeth Alice Louise, in the music room at Buckingham Palace in the presence of three British queens, past, present and future.

What would Victoria make of the way Anne handles the modern dilemma of being a royal princess in the seventies? Unlike her mother, Anne has always had one foot outside the royal goldfish bowl. In many respects, she has lived the life of a wealthy upper-class girl of her age. At thirteen, she was sent to boarding school – finishing with six O-levels and two A-levels; she drives her own fast car, sails and rides, belongs to trendy London clubs and is often seen at fashionable restaurants and discothèques. She is outspoken, unpredictable, energetic. She has driven a London bus and a Chieftain tank; has been stopped for speeding on the motorway and is frequently spontaneously rude to the Press.

She has collected some unlikely titles for royalty. At nineteen, she was voted Teenager of the Year; at twenty-one she was named BBC TV Sports Personality; in 1971 she became the first member of a horsy royal family to bag an equestrian title, when she won the European individual three-day event at Burghley. And she is certainly the first royal bride ever to have been described by the best man as 'a smashing bird'!

Yet royalty is all about her, 'like the red cordon round the furniture in a stately home', as someone described her at Cowes. When the occasion demands it, she can look regal, with something of her great-grandmother, Queen Mary, about her bearing and her cast of features. The dumpy teenager has grown into a very pretty girl, with a slim and graceful figure, long honey-blonde hair, keen blue eyes and her mother's lovely complexion – she's infinitely more attractive than her photographs give her credit for.

In jeans and a sweater, sailing a boat or exercising a horse, she is clearly her father's daughter, with the same down-to-earth quality, vitality and impatience. Like him, she does not suffer fools gladly – in an unprecedented TV interview with her fiancé two days before the wedding, she parried a fatuous question about cooking breakfast and sewing on buttons by snapping acidly: 'I'm not totally useless, I was quite well educated one way and another.' She seemed on edge and on the defensive, but it was a royal 'first' and though it was not exactly trial by television, it was not quite the cosy atmosphere of the Queen's Christmas message.

The curly-haired two-year-old who romped through her mother's coronation grew up to be the tomboy of the family. It was she who climbed trees and rode fearlessly, since the Queen first placed her on a fat Shetland pony at the age of three. Riding has provided her with an opportunity for being herself, for dressing informally, for meeting people outside royal circles on a personal basis and for competing in a world where courage, skill and training matter more than being a princess. Eventing is a tough, competitive sport: she's good at it, and proud of the fact. It is not surprising, therefore, that she should have found a husband from this world rather than from the diminishing list of less and less eligible princes.

'They could almost have been computer-dated' is supposed to have been the Queen Mother's up-to-date comment on the engagement. And it was with the Queen Mother that Anne first met Mark at a post-Olympic party in the Whitbread Cellar in the City in 1968. 'My grandmother took me, she thought I might find it rather fun and I, as a beginner at eventing was very overawed with all these grand people.' A candid comment from a queen's daughter!

But though Anne and Mark went on meeting at horse trials, she seemed more interested in Olympic gold medallist and show jumper Richard Meade. Until one evening in 1972. It happened during the horse trials at Crookham, in Hampshire. The Princess was invited to a dinner dance; Mark was asked to partner her and they spent most of the evening together, talking and dancing. The love affair matured slowly, against a background of horse flesh and to the inevitable chatter of newspaper headlines. 'They were training together . . . Anne was looking after Mark's horse . . . Mark was riding the Queen's horse, Columbus . . . Anne was spending weekends at the Phillipses' country home . . .' Sometimes the Princess was recognised, but more often she strolled round the village in slacks and a headscarf and nobody gave her a second glance.

The Phillipses' sixteenth-century home, the Mount House, is a mellow family house, with chintz curtains, a pleasant garden and an assortment of dogs. It stands in two and a half acres, overlooking the church in the sleepy village of Great Somerford in Wiltshire. There Mark's parents live the comfortable life of a British upper-middle-class family. They have no title and no great wealth, but they come from good yeoman stock.

On his mother's side, the Tiarks, there is even a tenuous link with the Royal Family – Mark's grandfather was an ADC to King George VI and genealogists have traced the family back to King Edward I.

On the Phillips side, there is a pleasant background of the proletariat making good. Mark's great-great-grandfather was a coal miner who did well, becoming a mine manager and finally a mine-owner and landowner. Mark's father may have associations with the humble sausage – he is a director of Wall's – but it is on a suitably elevated level and after all what is more reassuringly British and classless than a banger?

Mark grew up on the family farm at Tewkesbury, in an atmosphere strongly redolent of horses, and was riding his first pony at the age of two. After prep school he went to Marlborough, where he distinguished himself more for his athletic prowess than for his academic achievements. In 1967 he enlisted as a rifleman in the Green Jackets, won a place at Sandhurst and became an officer cadet. He is back there now as an instructor and a captain in an old and distinguished regiment, the 1st, the Queen's Dragoons, raised by James II in 1685.

It was not an easy courtship for the dragoon and his princess, their every step dogged by the Press. But they found ways to meet in private, often spending quiet weekends at the Catterick home of Mark's commanding officer, and once they were smuggled past reporters in a horse box. When Mark had to rejoin his regiment in Germany, it was Anne who drove him to the docks at Harwich and kissed him goodbye on the quay. The rumours really started to fly then with the Princess tartly issuing her own denials: 'There is no

88

romance and there are no grounds for these rumours of a romance between us.' Meanwhile, back at the Palace, a bouquet of three dozen red roses and lilies of the valley had arrived for Anne from Germany, where, for his part, Mark was saying firmly, 'Princess Anne and I are just good friends with a common interest.'

Five weeks later, the Court Circular announced the engagement between the Queen's 'beloved daughter' and the son of Mr and Mrs Peter Phillips.

The couple gave a Press conference and defended their denials. In March 'I was a confirmed bachelor, I had no intention of getting married,' Mark explained shyly; it had happened after the Badminton Horse Trials, but they had kept it secret for six weeks, perhaps to savour that commodity rare in royal circles – a little privacy.

The Princess had hoped for a simple wedding, but she got the full royal treatment – the Abbey, the Archbishop, the Household Cavalry, the fairy-tale coaches and the whole event relayed in full colour by satellite to a curious world.

But there were small touches of informality. The wedding dress was commissioned from the off-the-peg house of Susan Small where Anne buys most of her clothes. And the Princess chose to have just one bridesmaid and a page – her cousin, nine-year-old Lady Sarah Armstrong-Jones, and her youngest brother, Prince Edward, also nine. 'Having seen yards of uncontrollable children wandering up and down the aisle, I really thought it was so much easier and tidier just to have the two,' she explained.

Instead of the formal reception for visiting royalty which preceded their own wedding, the Queen and Prince Philip gave a dance for the many friends of the young couple who could not be invited to the wedding because there was no room in the Abbey.

In the Palace's gold and crimson ballroom, Anne, looking radiant in yellow silk, opened the dancing with Mark to the tune of 'The Loveliest Night of the Year'. At her request, they were alone on the dance floor for a minute or two before the guests joined in. Before the dance 100 of the guests were invited to a dinner party. They included Prince Rainier and Princess Grace of Monaco (he was the only reigning head of state at the wedding), ex-King Constantine of Greece and his wife Anne Marie of Denmark, Crown Prince Harald of Norway and his Princess, Franco's heir apparent Prince Juan Carlos of Spain and his wife, Princess Sophie of Greece. The family included uncle Dickie Mountbatten, Mr and Mrs Peter Phillips and a sprightly ninety-year-old who must have remembered more royal weddings than anyone else there, Princess Alice, Countess of Athlone.

Mark's last fling as a bachelor was held at a small restaurant in Notting Hill Gate – hardly royal territory. It was organised and paid for by his friend and best man, Captain Eric Grounds. Fourteen dragoon officers ate roast duck and drank champagne at a party which went on until the early hours. The champagne was on the house – earned by Mark's ability to down a bottle in three minutes, stopping only for breath.

The wedding gifts were the object of the usual curiosity and were the same juxtaposition of the grand with the unwanted and the bizarre which every bride and groom dread. The family came up trumps – there was an aquamarine and diamond tiara from the Queen Mother; diamond earrings and a gold brooch from the Queen; a Chippendale writing desk from Prince Philip; and a simple mirror, obviously hand-picked, from Prince Edward. Edward Heath sent a useful Persian carpet.

Perhaps mindful of the size of royal wardrobes, Princess Margaretha of Sweden sent eight dozen coat hangers, and the couple received endless horse brasses, horse prints, plaques of horse and rider and copies of the *Encyclopaedia of the Horse*, with enough saddles, horse blankets, fetlock straps and shin pads to equip a cavalry regiment.

Fittingly, as the Princess is President of the Save the Children Fund, there were small gifts from children – three felt mice, a bulldog clip, a toffee from two small girls, which went on display with the silver and the jewellery, dutifully catalogued as 'confectionery'.

The royal wedding cake was a gift too, from the Army Catering Corps. Taller and heavier than the Princess, it stood 5ft 8in high, weighed 144lb, and contained 84 eggs, 10lb of butter, 2 bottles of brandy, 53lb of fruit and 2 secret ingredients. The cook used a light hand with the marzipan, as the Princess dislikes it.

Like her mother, Anne was a November bride. The day she

chose, the 14th, was Prince Charles's twenty-fifth birthday and the sixty-ninth birthday of the Archbishop of Canterbury, Dr Ramsay, who was officiating at his last royal wedding before retiring. It was a perfect autumn day, cool and crisp, the golden leaves brilliant against a bright blue sky, the sun striking sparks from the glass coaches and the Household Cavalry's helmets and breastplates.

Over 2,000 members of the three armed services were involved in the ceremonial and 1,400 policemen provided the strictest security control ever found necessary for a British royal wedding. It was a sad reflection of the times that people who had camped out all night had their vacuum flasks and sandwich tins confiscated in the search for bombs. Inside the Abbey, specially trained dogs sniffed round hallowed corners, and security men were discreetly stationed behind pillars and statues.

The bridegroom had spent his last night as a bachelor with his best man at the Cavalry Club, where, we are told, he breakfasted at 9.30 on bacon and eggs, followed by a steadying whisky before he left for the Abbey. There he changed into his new uniform – £250 worth of scarlet and gold tunic with blue velvet collar and cuffs and skin-tight trousers. At his side, his best man, similarly attired, wore the wedding ring of Welsh gold on his little finger, as the uniform has no pockets.

Soon after 11, the first coach left the Palace, the pretty newly-restored Scottish State Coach with a family party – the Queen, the Queen Mother, the Prince of Wales and Prince Andrew. The Queen, slim and youthful-looking in bright blue, seemed happy and relaxed and was obviously enjoying her daughter's wedding. They were followed by the Irish State Coach, with Princess Margaret, Lord Snowdon and their son Viscount Linley. The young bridesmaid and page rode together in a state landau, waving at the crowds. A loud cheer announced the first glimpse of the bride's procession, Princess Anne and her father in the Glass Coach, first used by King George V for his coronation, and drawn by four greys.

At the Abbey, the waiting clergy included relatives of both bride and groom: the Right Rev Geoffrey Tiarks, Bishop of Maidstone, Mark's cousin, and the Rev Andrew Elphinstone, first cousin of the Queen and a godfather of the Princess. There was no wedding march, the bride's arrival being heralded by a fanfare from the regimental trumpeters of the bridegroom's regiment. At the sound, the 1,500 guests in the Abbey craned their necks for their first sight of the Princess. This was the moment they had waited for, the twenty-five members of foreign royalty, the peers and diplomats, the MPs and the friends, and from Great Somerford the Phillipses' daily and the village blacksmith who must have shod a horse or two for Anne and Mark.

The bride looked cool, lovely and very feminine, a veritable medieval princess, in her dress of white silk, high-necked and delicately pintucked to show off her tiny waist. The main feature of the dress was the huge trumpet sleeves, tucked to the elbow and flared out over finely pleated chiffon. The neckline and shoulders were embroidered with pearls, and pearls and silver thread picked out a design of flowers on the long, pure silk gauze train.

The Princess wore something old – the same diamond tiara which her mother had worn on her wedding day – but what a world of difference between this cool and confident young bride chatting with her handsome father and the shy, tremulous quality which radiated from the young Elizabeth on that November day in 1947! The likeness with Prince Philip, very dashing in the uniform of a field-marshal, was very striking as they walked down the aisle, while the choir sang 'Glorious Things of Thee are Spoken'.

The bouquet of white roses and lily of the valley, with a sprig of white Scottish heather for luck and a piece of myrtle grown from Queen Victoria's bouquet for sentiment, was handed to Lady Sarah Armstrong-Jones. She looked like a young Juliet, in a white silk pinafore dress with lattice-work sleeves and a small white cap, standing very poised by Prince Edward, solemn in his kilt and black velvet jacket.

Anne exchanged her vows where her mother and grandmother had knelt before her – the sacrarium of the Abbey, with its thirteenth-century Roman mosaic floor, its gold screens and tapestries and the display of glittering Abbey plate. Because the Royal Family traditionally sit on the right, the usual wedding seating arrangement was reversed and the bride's guests sat on the right of the Abbey.

If the Phillips clan on the left were overawed by the occasion, there was no sign of it – not the slightest quiver in the ostrich feather topping Mrs Phillips's eau-de-nil outfit or her daughter's extraordinary pink bonnet, rather like a circus equestrienne's.

After the signing of the registers, and the deep curtsey to the Queen, Captain and Mrs Mark Phillips cantered down the aisle to the strains of Strauss's 'Radetsky March' – the regimental march of the Dragoon Guards – an operetta-like finale to the wedding of the fair-haired Princess and the dashing Dragoon; as one woman in the crowd told a reporter, 'If I'm down in the dumps I go to the theatre to cheer up. That's just like today.'

But despite the pageantry, what was miraculously preserved and transmitted to millions of viewers was the personal flavour of a family wedding. The Queen and Prince Philip were marrying off their only daughter to a handsome young man who rides well and loves horses and dogs, and they were enjoying it all. Even the customary balcony appearance at 1.30 was more informal, with less hand waving and more laughter, and, one sensed, family jokes.

The wedding breakfast was a relatively simple three-course menu:

Oeufs Drumkilbo (eggs, lobster, shrimps and tomato in a light mayonnaise)

Perdeau en cocotte bonne femme, petits pois au beurre, chou-fleur glacé, pommes nouvelles (partridge with a garnish of button onions, mushrooms and bacon rolls, served with buttered peas, glazed cauliflower and new potatoes)

Salad and Bombe Royale (peppermint bombe with grated chocolate inside)

And the wines:

Niersteiner 1969, Château Mouton Rothschild 1955, Heidsieck Dry 1966 and Dow's Port 1955

The guests included both families, the Archbishop of Canterbury and Mrs Ramsay, the Dean of Westminster, Dr Eric Abbott. The best man sat at an adjoining table with the bridesmaid and Prince Andrew.

At approximately 4 o'clock an open carriage drove out of the Palace gates with the bride and her husband. The Princess wore a romantic blue velvet coat with white mink collar, cuffs and a matching white mink hat. They were driven to the Royal Hospital, Chelsea, where a maroon Rolls Royce waited to whisk them to a secret destination for the night – Princess Alexandra's lovely house in Richmond Park, Thatched House Lodge. The Ogilvys, who were attending Prince Charles's twenty-fifth birthday party at Buckingham Palace, spent the night at the Palace, to leave the newly-weds in complete privacy.

The next morning the couple flew from Heathrow to Barbados to join the royal yacht *Britannia* for a three-week Caribbean cruise. This was followed by their first public engagement as a married couple – a visit to Ecuador, Colombia, Jamaica and Montserrat. It was not all work; there was a lot of fun, especially when, to the sound of exploding fire crackers, they joined the people of Quito dancing and singing in the streets to celebrate the founding of their city by the Conquistadors. There was a picnic high up on the slopes of Mount Cotopaxi in the Ecuadorean Andes, where Anne and Mark wore bright ponchos, bought in a street market in the dusty village of Saquisily. While they bargained, an ecstatic announcer bellowed into a loudspeaker the information that 'the Queen of London and her husband the Prince Philips Marks' were honouring their humble shopping centre.

Back home, suntanned and obviously happy, they set up home in married quarters in Sandhurst – their billet, Oak Grove House, a five-bedroomed Georgian house, leased to Mark for £8 a week, and treated to a £25,000 face-lift amid much public controversy. Here the couple are looked after by a nineteen-year-old cook-housekeeper, helped by local dailies and a butler-valet for Mark.

And so they settled down to the ordinary routine of one of the least ordinary families in the world.

NOTES and REFERENCES

Chapter 1   Victoria and 'Dearest Albert'

1 Cecil Woodham-Smith, *Queen Victoria, Her Life and Times* (1972), p. 37.
2 Elizabeth Longford, *Victoria R.I.* (1964), p. 130.
3 *The Letters of Queen Victoria, 1837–1861*, ed. A. C. Benson and Viscount Esher (1907), p. 15.
4 Dormer Creston, *The Youthful Queen Victoria* (1952), p. 133.
5 Ibid., p. 167.
6 Ibid., p. 170.
7 Ibid., p. 339.
8 *Queen Victoria, Her Life and Times*, p. 119.
9 *The Letters of Queen Victoria, 1837–1861*, p. 62.
10 *The Youthful Queen Victoria*, p. 201.
11 *Queen Victoria, Her Life and Times*, p. 122.
12 *The Letters of Queen Victoria, 1837–1861*, p. 62.
13 *Queen Victoria, Her Life and Times*, p. 122.
14 *The Girlhood of Queen Victoria*, ed. Viscount Esher (1912), p. 144.
15 *Victoria, Albert and Mrs Stevenson: The Letters of Sallie Coles Stevenson*, ed. Edward Boykin (1957), p. 77.
16 *The Youthful Queen Victoria*, p. 262.
17 *Queen Victoria, Her Life and Times*, p. 140.
18 Ibid., p. 176.
19 *The Youthful Queen Victoria*, p. 319.
20 *Queen Victoria, Her Life and Times*, p. 186.
21 Ibid., p. 162.
22 Ibid., p. 176.
23 *The Letters of Queen Victoria, 1837–1861*, p. 224.
24 Ibid., p. 235.
25 *The Youthful Queen Victoria*, p. 423.
26 *The Letters of Queen Victoria, 1837–1861*, p. 237.
27 Roger Fulford, *The Prince Consort* (1949), p. 43.
28 *Queen Victoria, Her Life and Times*, p. 184.
29 *The Letters of Queen Victoria, 1837–1861*, p. 239.

30 *Queen Victoria, Her Life and Times,* p. 190.
31 Ibid., p. 191.
32 *The Youthful Queen Victoria,* p. 432.
33 *The German Bridegroom,* a satire by the Hon. J. W. [Southgate] (1840).
34 *The Youthful Queen Victoria,* p. 434.
35 *The Letters of Queen Victoria, 1837–1861,* p. 254.
36 Ibid., p. 269.
37 *The Youthful Queen Victoria,* pp. 431, 432.
38 *The Letters of Queen Victoria, 1837–1861,* p. 267.
39 *The Youthful Queen Victoria,* p. 442.
40 *Victoria, R.I.,* p. 142.
41 *The Letters of Queen Victoria, 1837–1861,* p. 273.
42 *The Youthful Queen Victoria,* p. 446.
43 *Victoria, Albert and Mrs Stevenson,* p. 244.
44 *The Youthful Queen Victoria,* p. 460.
45 G. Barnett Smith, *The Life of Queen Victoria* (1897), pp. 62, 63.
46 *The Youthful Queen Victoria,* p. 461.
47 Ibid.
48 *Queen Victoria, Her Life and Times,* p. 205.
49 Ibid.
50 Ibid.
51 Ibid., p. 206.
52 *Victoria R.I.,* p. 144.
53 *The Letters of Queen Victoria, 1837–1861,* p. 274.

Chapter 2   Queen Alexandra

1 Georgina Battiscombe, *Queen Alexandra* (1969), p. 7.
2 *Dearest Mama: Letters between Queen Victoria and the Crown Princess of Prussia, 1861–1864,* ed. Roger Fulford (1968), p. 173.
3 Philip Magnus, *Edward VII* (1964), p. 19.
4 Ibid., p. 14.
5 Ibid., p. 32.
6 Ibid., p. 30.
7 Ibid., p. 32.
8 Ibid., p. 41.
9 *Queen Alexandra,* p. 17.
10 Ibid., p. 19.
11 Ibid.
12 *Edward VII,* p. 46.

13 *Queen Alexandra*, p. 21.
14 *Edward VII*, p. 49.
15 Ibid.
16 Ibid., p. 51.
17 Ibid., p. 52.
18 Ibid.
19 *Dearest Mama*, p. 38.
20 *Edward VII*, p. 58.
21 Ibid.
22 *Queen Alexandra*, p. 38.
23 *Edward VII*, p. 60.
24 *Dearest Mama*, p. 142.
25 Ibid., p. 164.
26 Ibid., p. 168.
27 Ibid., p. 172.
28 *Edward VII*, p. 66.
29 Ibid., p. 67.
30 *My Dear Duchess: Social and Political Letters to the Duchess of Manchester, 1858–1869*, ed. A. L. Kennedy (1956), p. 214.
31 *Illustrated London News* (14 March 1863).
32 *My Dear Duchess*, p. 214.
33 Ibid.
34 Ibid., p. 210.
35 *Queen Alexandra*, p. 50.
36 Ibid.
37 Geoffrey Wakeford, *Thirty Years a Queen* (1968), p. 149.

Chapter 3   Georgie and Princess May

1 James Hope-Hennessy, *Queen Mary* (1959), p. 25.
2 Ibid., p. 38.
3 Ibid., p. 56.
4 Ibid., p. 164.
5 Ibid., p. 187.
6 Ibid., p. 195.
7 Ibid., p. 207.
8 Ibid.
9 Ibid., p. 210.
10 *The Letters of Queen Victoria*, Vol II: *A Selection from Her Majesty's Correspondence and Journal between 1886 and 1901*, ed. George Earle Buckle (1931), p. 81.

11 Ibid., p. 82.
12 *Queen Mary*, p. 215.
13 *The Letters of Queen Victoria*, Vol II, p. 92.
14 Ibid., p. 92; *Edward VII*, p. 239.
15 *Queen Mary*, p. 225.
16 Ibid., p. 249.
17 Ibid., p. 255.
18 Harold Nicolson, *King George V* (1952), p. 49.
19 Ibid., p. 50.
20 *Queen Mary*, p. 261.
21 Ibid., p. 262.
22 *The Letters of Queen Victoria*, Vol II, p. 272.
23 *Queen Mary*, p. 266.
24 *The Letters of Queen Victoria*, Vol II, p. 273.
25 Ibid.
26 Ibid.
27 Ibid.
28 *Queen Mary*, p. 280.
29 Ibid., p. 417.

Chapter 4   Elizabeth and the Duke of York

1 John W. Wheeler-Bennett, *King George VI* (1958), p. 146.
2 Dorothy Laird, *Queen Elizabeth the Queen Mother and Her Support to the Throne during Four Reigns* (1966), p. 51.
3 Geoffrey Wakeford, *Thirty Years a Queen* (1968), p. 42.
4 *King George VI*, p. 18.
5 Ibid., p. 39.
6 Ibid., p. 59.
7 Ibid., p. 58.
8 *Thirty Years a Queen*, p. 47.
9 Ibid., p. 48.
10 Ibid., p. 59.
11 *King George VI*, p. 150.
12 *Thirty Years a Queen*, p. 22.
13 *King George VI*, p. 150.
14 Ibid., p. 151.
15 Lady Cynthia Asquith, *The Duchess of York* (1928), p. 166.
16 *Thirty Years a Queen*, p. 29.
17 *King George VI*, p. 154.
18 Ibid., p. 155.

Chapter 5   Elizabeth and Philip

1 James Pope-Hennessy, *Queen Mary* (1959), p. 530.
2 Ibid., p. 594.
3 John W. Wheeler-Bennett, *King George VI* (1958), p. 626.
4 Ibid., p. 749.
5 *Queen Mary*, p. 615.
6 *King George VI*, p. 753.
7 *Queen Mary*, p. 616.
8 *King George VI*, p. 754.
9 Ibid., p. 755.

Chapter 6   Princess Margaret

1 Geoffrey Wakeford, *Thirty Years a Queen* (1968), p. 109.
2 Ibid., p. 111.
3 Ibid., p. 121.

Chapter 7   Princess Anne

1 Princess Marie Louise, *My Memories of Six Reigns* (1956), p. 315.

BIBLIOGRAPHY

Asquith, Lady Cynthia. *The Duchess of York*. Hutchinson, 1928.

Barnett Smith, G. *The Life of Queen Victoria*. Routledge, 1897.

Battiscombe, Georgina. *Queen Alexandra*. Constable, 1969.

Benson, A. C., and Esher, Viscount (eds). *The Letters of Queen Victoria, 1837–1861*. John Murray, 1907.

Boothroyd, Basil. *Prince Philip*. Longmans, 1971.

Boykin, Edward (ed.). *Victoria, Albert and Mrs Stevenson: The Letters of Sallie Coles Stevenson*. Frederick Muller, 1957.

Buckle, G. E. (ed.). *The Letters of Queen Victoria*, Vol II: *A Selection from Her Majesty's Correspondence and Journal between 1886 and 1901*. John Murray, 1931.

Creston, Dormer. *The Youthful Queen Victoria*. Macmillan, 1952.

Duff, David. *Albert and Victoria*. Frederick Muller, 1972.

Esher, Viscount (ed.). *The Girlhood of Queen Victoria*, a selection from the Queen's diaries, 1832–40. John Murray, 1912.

Fulford, Roger. *The Prince Consort*. Macmillan, 1949.

——. *Hanover to Windsor*. Batsford, 1960.

——. (ed.). *Dearest Mama: Letters between Queen Victoria and the Crown Princess of Prussia, 1861–1864*. Evans, 1968.

Kennedy, A. L. (ed.). *My Dear Duchess: Social and Political Letters to the Duchess of Manchester, 1858–1869*. John Murray, 1956.

Laird, Dorothy. *Queen Elizabeth the Queen Mother and Her Support to the Throne during Four Reigns*. Hodder & Stoughton, 1966.

Longford, Elizabeth, *Victoria R.I.* Weidenfeld & Nicolson, 1964.

Magnus, Philip. *Edward VII*. John Murray, 1964.

Marie Louise, Princess. *My Memories of Six Reigns*. Evans, 1956.

Nicolson, Harold. *King George V*. Constable, 1952.

Pope-Hennessy, James. *Queen Mary*. Allen & Unwin, 1959.

Strachey, Lytton. *Queen Victoria*. Chatto & Windus, 1921.

Wakeford, Geoffrey. *Thirty Years a Queen*. Robert Hale, 1968.

Wheeler-Bennett, John W. *King George VI*. Macmillan, 1958.

Woodham-Smith, Cecil. *Queen Victoria, Her Life and Times*. Hamish Hamilton, 1972.

THE ROYAL HOUSE OF WINDSOR
Elizabeth Longford

In 1917 King George V changed his name from the German-sounding Saxe-Coburg in response to the intense anti-German feelings which marked public opinion during the war years. Thus the Windsors, the family name of the present Royal House, came into being.

The first Windsor reigned during the agonies of the Great War and lived on to become a much-loved father to his subjects in a far-flung empire. Then followed the brief but dramatic reign of Edward VIII, ending in the trauma of abdication and leading to the accession of his younger brother. Shy and withdrawn where Edward had been extrovert and dashing, George VI found an ideal consort in Elizabeth Bowes-Lyon and rose to become, like his father, a beloved figure and a symbol of the nation's unity in war.

When George died in 1952 he was succeeded by Elizabeth, his twenty-five-year-old daughter. She faced the problem of an expectant nation acclaiming with highest hopes the 'new Elizabethan age'. In establishing a uniquely informal style of monarchy, this Queen has made herself more accessible, certainly more widely known, than any sovereign in the nation's history.

'Lady Longford portrays King George V and his three successors with clarity, learning and understanding of character. The anecdotes moreover are amusing, the illustrations lavish, the considerations on our monarchy today thoughtful' – *Sunday Times*

Illustrated

0 7221 5599 9   £2·50

THE SUN KING
Nancy Mitford

The Sun King is a magnificent recreation of the reign of Louis XIV and a brilliant evocation of the hunting lodge at Versailles which he transformed into the greatest palace in Europe. Nancy Mitford describes the daily life of the King, the court and the government during the years of France's zenith in military power and artistic achievement. She follows the gradual creation of the palace, the complex intrigues of the court – and the course of Louis's love affairs, culminating in his secret marriage to Madame de Maintenon.

'This gay, engaging yet wonderfully penetrating study of Louis XIV in the setting of his own Versailles . . . A *tour de force*' – *Punch*

Illustrated

0 7221 6140 9

£2·50

MADAME DE POMPADOUR
Nancy Mitford

'High rouged, unfortunate female,' said Carlyle of Madame de Pompadour, 'of whom it is not proper to speak without necessity.' Happily Nancy Mitford has felt no such reticence in presenting this glittering portrait of the mistress of Louis XV.

In a lively combination of history and character study the author describes the life of Madame de Pompadour, her rise to power and her twenty-year reign as the King's mistress. She paints a vivid picture of the court, for years the artistic and intellectual centre of Europe, and skilfully untangles the complicated threads of politics at home and abroad.

'A shrewdly well-balanced, witty and sympathetic portrait' – *Punch*

Illustrated

0 7221 6141 7

£2·50

All Sphere Books are available at your bookshop or
newsagent, or can be ordered from the following address:
Sphere Books, Cash Sales Department,
P.O. Box 11, Falmouth, Cornwall.

Please send cheque or postal order (no currency), and allow
19p for postage and packing for the first book plus 9p
per copy for each additional book ordered up to a
maximum charge of 73p in U.K.

Customers in Eire and B.F.P.O. please allow 19p for
postage and packing for the first book plus 9p per copy
for the next 6 books, thereafter 3p per book.

Overseas customers please allow 20p for postage and
packing for the first book and 10p per copy for each
additional book.